The Cruciform Way

A Steady Cadence of Christ for Life

Volume I

Reverend Christopher I. Thoma

Angels' Portion Books

Text © 2021 by Christopher I. Thoma

FIRST EDITION

Angels' Portion Books
AngelsPortion.com

Cover design and layout: APB
Cover Image: Conger Design
For more information visit:
https://angelsportion.com & https://cruciformstuff.com

Thoma, Christopher I., 1972—
The Cruciform Way: A Steady Cadence of Christ for Life, Volume I
ISBN-13: 978-1-7367051-0-0
Printed in the United States of America.

For the People of God at
Our Savior Evangelical Lutheran Church & School
Hartland, Michigan

✝

You are worth every effort.

CONTENTS

TRINITY

INTRODUCTION

T he title of this volume, *The Cruciform Way*, gives a hint to its purpose. It is a Christological commentary—or a devotional if you will—on everything that is "life."

Each of the individual observations you'll discover here have first served as an in-the-moment, thought-filled, Gospel-induced introduction for a newsletter that I send out by email to the members of my congregation each and every week.

Yes, I write and send a newsletter every week.

Yes, this is often a monumental task.

Yes, it is absolutely worth every bit of the effort.

Keeping a steady cadence of communication with the people in my care is something I consider to be of high importance, and with the various avenues provided by email and social media, the reach and potency for such things become all the more amplified.

I've been doing this for several years, and the results have far exceeded what I could have ever imagined. A renaissance of commitment as members of a Christian family has occurred, and with that, good things continue to happen. Namely, I've seen God's people engaging, conversing, and coming to a much deeper and more vivid understanding of who they are in Christ. Even better, the togetherness that continues to develop has proven itself muscular for tackling some fairly formidable challenges as a community.

In short, I believe it has helped my congregation grow in faithfulness to Christ and in loving service for the neighbor.

Just so you know, not all of the eNews portions I've ever written are shared here. I exclude some because they are far too intimate to the membership. Of the ones that I do share with you for devotional purposes, of course, I've excluded information about potlucks, weekday confirmation, and such. As I said, I'm only giving the devotional words—or as the tagline for this volume reveals: *A Steady Cadence of Christ for Life.*

By the way, you should know that I rarely planned what was written and shared. I would scribe whatever came to mind at the moment. Even so, I won't deny that everything written serves according to the grander plan I mentioned before—which is simply to give a steady stream of God's Word to the people in my care.

Sometimes the stream stings more than it soothes. Sometimes it's a breath of fresh air sweeping through a dank and stale mood. But no matter what you find in the pages that follow, all are things that Christians should be speaking to one another with regularity. I share them here with you in devotional form, and I do so according to the hope that they can, and will, serve beyond the borders of my little church and school in Hartland, Michigan.

In Jesus,
Reverend Christopher I. Thoma ✝

ADVENT & CHRISTMAS

Advent Recalibration

Then shall your light break forth like the dawn, and your healing shall spring up speedily; your righteousness shall go before you; the glory of the LORD shall be your rear guard. —Isaiah 58:8

The season of Advent has arrived. The Christian Church Year begins anew.

Of course for many, Advent is a favorite time. This is true not only as we find ourselves brimming with excitement for Christmas—the bright-beaming décor and the colorful adornments—but because we're conscious of the season's purpose, and we know the deeper, recalibrating consequence Advent is in place to deliver into our lives.

It sets a very important pace for the whole Church Year.

If Advent were just about getting ready for Christmas, the season's prescribed readings would betray such an inclination. But they don't. They're fuller than that. Advent's very first Gospel reading—the Palm Sunday reading from Matthew 21—is proof. Starting off the new Church Year by going straight to Palm Sunday teaches that we live our lives as Christians in a perpetual Holy Week. Everything and anything we do and say from the First Sunday in Advent to the Last Sunday in the Church Year is in motion toward the cross of Jesus Christ.

Advent helps to join our hopeful anticipation of the evening long ago when the Savior of the world was born to the dreadful day on Golgotha's hill when that same Savior went into the darkness of sin and was crucified, winning our confidence against the looming reality of the day when Jesus will return and the world will be judged.

5

Advent preaches both the first and the second comings of Christ.

With such preaching, along comes the Law and Gospel, sin and grace, real warning, and real hope that humans need. I suppose many church-goers, like the world around us, might prefer we remain in the frothier upland of "Jingle Bells" and such. But Advent digs deeper than that. It's honest. It doesn't hold back on the harder news of our spiritual blindness. Advent more than remembers the sightlessness of the sin-nature. The Word of God is clear that without the recreating work of the Holy Spirit by the Gospel message of Christ's life, death, and resurrection, the Savior is unknowable to us (John 1:9-10). In fact, by default, according to the sin-nature, we're not even the least bit interested in knowing Him (Romans 8:7). We haven't the slightest morsel of interest for seeking the love that God is bringing. But that right there is perhaps a wonderful glimpse of the beautifully balanced gilding of Advent. Shakespeare said it well. "Love sought is good, but giv'n unsought is better" (*Twelfth Night*, III, i, 170). We did not seek the Lord's love, but He reached to us in Jesus and gave it anyway.

When this message has its way with us, it changes the nature of things. The blur of sorts remains, but now as believers, it isn't one that doesn't know what's coming. It isn't one that doesn't know where to discover this hope that helps us see clearly. We're waiting for Christmas. We can't see it yet, but we know it's coming. And when it arrives, we know the substance of the celebration. We're waiting for Holy Week. We're not there yet, but we know it will arrive. When it does, we know its innermost drive. We're always watching for the Last Day. It hasn't arrived yet. But still, when it does, we'll be ready.

"Your light will break forth like the dawn," the Prophet Isaiah says of these things. Paul speaks similarly when he describes us as looking through a dimly lit glass (1 Corinthians 13:12). Both Isaiah and Paul mean to say that even as we are waiting, by faith in Christ, each of these moments already sits at the edge of arrival—and we're ready.

Believers know these things. It's craziness to the world. But for us, everything is different now.

I feel bad for churches that don't use lectionaries or follow the Church Year calendar. Those churches are more likely to miss these imports of Advent. They're more likely to get immersed in a pastor's favorite topics, being fed anecdote after useless anecdote about anything and everything except the determined preaching of Christ crucified for transgressions—which is the heartbeat of the whole Church Year and its Lectionary, the first of its cadence beginning with Advent.

A four-week sermon series on how to be a better tither at Christmas just seems to miss the mark.

By the way, since I mentioned Paul and his dimly lit glass, and thinking on a church that knows how to observe Advent in comparison to one that doesn't, all of this sort of reminds me of a scene from Lewis Carroll's *Through the Looking Glass*:

> "I see nobody on the road," said Alice.
> "I only wish I had such eyes," the King remarked in a fretful tone. "To be able to see Nobody! And at that distance, too! Why, it's as much as I can do to see real people by this light!"

The scene above might not be the tightest fit, but it did come to mind while typing. Even if only slightly, it reveals that while we and the world might be seeing the same things, we have completely dissimilar interpretations.

And so, in the end, what's the message here? I guess boiling it down, consider this visitation with the topics of Advent, the Church Year, and the prescribed readings of the Lectionary as an encouragement to go to church. Don't just make plans for Christmas. Immerse yourself in Advent, too. You need what the season offers—perhaps more than you might've been taught to know.

✠

I'd Like to Tell You a Story

In my distress I called to the LORD, and he answered me. —Psalm 120:1

I'd like to tell you a story. I've been given permission to tell it for your benefit. In one sense, you may already know the tale's beginning, because it is for you a telling of familiar things.

What I'm about to describe took place mid-morning. Even at 9:00 AM, the December sky was successfully holding back the sun's exuberance, leaving a pre-dawn feeling.

Through my office window, I saw the counterpart to my morning meeting making her way from the parking lot to the church doors. I'd promised her the evening before following the Advent service that I'd have coffee ready and waiting when she arrived, and so I reached for and dropped a K-cup into my Keurig. A newly washed mug was already in waiting below. The reservoir was empty, so it took a quick moment to fill it. In an instant, the coffee was flowing. As it did, I was out and down the office hallway toward the darkened entryway searching for my guest.

I didn't see her at first, although admittedly, I wasn't wearing my glasses. Assuming she may have taken a sideway into the restroom, I stood near the door to the offices. The day school children—all but a few of the 131 of them—were already in the church nave, gathered at the chancel and practicing for the Children's Christmas service only a few weeks away. They were rehearsing the final hymn, a masterfully orchestrated rendition of "Silent Night," which, if you've ever been to this particular service, then you know from experience there is little to compare. Because

I've participated in it for more than twenty years, I can see it now as I think about it.

The air is cool. The pews are filled. Family and friends sit compactly, yet happily. The nave and sanctuary are dimly lit. The candles throughout are fluttering, each child holding their own light. The Advent and Christmas décor are twinkling. The voices of the children hover above all of it on the pipe organ's melodies, as if the collective sound is coming from the heavens above, rather than the earth beneath.

It's always quite moving. Even rehearsals can carry a listener into divine spaces.

And then I saw my guest. Actually, no. I didn't see her. I heard her. She was barely a step from the entryway into the narthex—and she was crying. When she saw me approaching, she quickly began wiping the tears away only to begin sobbing more deeply.
"I needed this, today," she choked. "This is the first thing God gave me when I walked into this place this morning, and I truly needed it."

I was gentle with my words, making sure there was no shame at the moment. What she was doing was well and good in such a place. The Lord Himself knows I've been in similar situations. It can be overwhelming to hear the Gospel wrapped up and delivered in a way that truly communicates its divine origin. Tears are sometimes the soul's only reply.

We made our way down the hallway to my office. We spent the next hour sipping coffee and talking about a multitude of things. Amidst the confession of some harder histories, she noted there was no place she'd ever experienced like Our Savior. Having been raised Christian, she fell away in the years beyond her 18th birthday. But in these latter days, the need for something more had begun to overwhelm her.

She'd visited countless other churches—Roman Catholic, Lutheran, and others—still, she never found herself in a pew or stadium seat that actually communicated a station before eternity. She didn't say it with the precision that I intend to share right now, but again, I've been given permission to tell this story.

Her words crafted a narrative of far too many churches that, by their practices, imply the selling of religion. They sought to draw her closer to their ranks in the same ways the world might try—rock bands, screens, you name it. But in the swirling confusion of their seat-filling stratagem, they never could quite reach that part of her insides that was suffering. Their Gospel of justification before God always seemed wired to her ability to produce good deeds (which, for the wayward, can only default into terror), or by making a personal choice (and yet, how can a spiritual corpse—someone who knows oneself to be dead in trespasses and sins—choose Jesus?). Their sacraments were symbols, bringing very little consolation or certainty to a broken heart in need of more than referring to Jesus, but actually meeting with Him, and knowing He's there for her.

But at Our Savior Evangelical Lutheran Church in Hartland, Michigan, there was the sense of something unalike to these others.

"This church is so different," she said, repeatedly. "You're not like the other places I've been."

For her, the facility in which she was currently seated was different. For her, it not only had a sign that bore the title "church," but once inside, it seemed to be a dwelling place for someone or something so much more—something holy. And for of the several Sundays, she'd attended, of the people greeting and sitting beside her, none gave any sense to having been gathered by some sort of baiting impetus. None in the surrounding pews were there because of a lead guitarist with amazing skill. None were there because the pastors were stand-apart showmen among a sea of humdrum preachers. None were there to perform.

And she wasn't, either. She was in search of a place where the Divine might dwell, and she hoped that when she found Him, He'd take her back.

Stirring in this humble hope, she discovered herself sitting, standing, kneeling, praying, confessing, singing beside hundreds of others—acknowledged sinners, just like her—being carried along by a historic liturgy of solemnity and reverence. She was immersed in a service that, while strange in comparison to everything she'd collided with prior, she knew could only have been born from the same soil as countless generations of worshippers before her, a framework that began in the tiny house churches of the first century, built on the teachings of the Apostles and Prophets, all in place and sprouting up through the centuries to aim penitently grieving offenders to a gracious God who desires nothing more than to come and sit with them, to give them a Gospel of power that assures our deeds play no part in our salvation, a Gospel that takes hold of spiritual corpses and brings them to life, a Gospel that heals them and draws them close to the Son of God, Jesus Christ. This is a Gospel that heralds our God as one who holds no ill will for the sinner. He loves us. He forgives us. And He promises to be with us no matter how dark our days may be.

We left the conversation as only the Word of God could rightly describe, with the peace of God, which surpasses all understanding, guarding our hearts and minds in Christ Jesus (Philippians 4:7), and we made plans to meet on Thursdays at the same time to dig deeper into these things.

So, why I am sharing this with you, especially since in this postmodern, radically individualized age such situations happen frequently enough around here that they can barely be considered peculiar?

Chiefly, because I want to remind you of two things in particular.

First, be glad that there are churches that still deal in the more reverential realms of "holy." Be glad some churches keep the boundaries between the Church and the culture as crisply distinct as can be. Such places are in the divine business of building foundations for the long haul. Sure, people have the things they like, their preferences, their styles. To each his own, I suppose. "What works for some might not work for others," we'll hear repeated. Still, I wonder if perhaps that's a somewhat loaded response for protecting a church formed to oneself, a worship community created in one's own favorite and time-limited self-image. When you're gone, what's next? Whatever the next guy likes to do, I guess. True or not, at a minimum, be well aware that people know—they just know—when they're being entertained as opposed to being led into the substantive presence of a divine Someone who is far deeper than the wowing experientials indistinguishable from the world around them could ever reach. Sure, the self-image ways may speak of Jesus, but do they really point to Him? Do they really give nothing else but Him? Do they make the introduction? And will it last? Will it survive wars? Will it persist even among the prowling monsters of this age and the next? I wonder.

The second reason I share this returns us to the tears being shed in the Narthex. There's a reason Our Savior Evangelical Lutheran Church in Hartland, Michigan continues putting our time, treasure, and back-breaking muscle into a tuition-free, preschool through eighth-grade school. Not only is it an incomparable opportunity set before our community for getting kids out of the mind-bending education system that's shoving ungodliness down their tiny throats, but most importantly, it stands as a beacon for immersing generations of little ones in the only message that saves. From this, it becomes nothing less than a longstanding avenue for others to hear that same message through those same little ones. All a person has to do is walk in the doors, and it won't be long before the bright-beaming light of a Christian child will have its effect on the visitor.

Children are the consequential emissaries of a Christian school's existence.

Whether this work happens through the Children's Christmas service, among their neighborhood friends, or twenty years from now in a conversation with a fellow employee in the neighboring cubicle, Christian schools possess limitless Gospel horizons.

And so we put everything into our efforts here. We give it our best. We teach and preach of Christ. We train in Godliness and reverence, learning the rites and ceremonies, the creeds, the prayers, the hymnodies sung by the early churches and their people before being fed to lions. And we gather all of it up and cherish all of it together as the wonderfully sturdy gift from a loving God that it is.

It becomes a home base for the kind of Christianity that doesn't roll over, whether it's before the next big distracting, anthropocentric, contemporary trend, or it's an armed regiment sent by Caesar to snatch you away to your mortal doom.

☩

Connecting the Dots

At that time the disciples came to Jesus and asked, "Who, then, is the greatest in the kingdom of heaven?" He called a little child to him, and placed the child among them. And he said: "Truly I tell you, unless you change and become like little children, you will never enter the kingdom of heaven." —Matthew 18:1-3

If ever there was a season for sharing our stories with one another, it's the season of Advent. Advent is a season for gathering stories—the narratives of our lives. Even better, Advent leads the way as it ventures to gather up the accounts of the Bible—which are our stories, too—and it aims them at Jesus.

I like that.

I like that Advent plays by the all-important rule that Jesus is the key to understanding the Scriptures. If you don't approach the Bible through the lens of the Gospel, you won't be able to see the whole picture. Your connect-the-dot picture of a puppy will look more like a tornado of scribbles.

A big part of being a Christian is being able to connect the dots that no one else can. It means beholding this world's monsters stacking tragedy upon tragedy and knowing the deeper concern behind it all. It also means seeing our God laboring in the middle of all of it for our rescue through the person and work of His Son, Jesus Christ. It means being able to see Him through the fog—to see Him when and where the world can't.

Jesus said that would be the case for His believers. In John 14:19, He said that He was going away, and yet, even as the world wouldn't be able to see Him, we would.

Now, you may be thinking that I'm carrying this toward Christians beholding God in the gentle display of a mid-summer rain shower or the majestic grandeur of an Appalachian mountain range in winter. But that's not what Jesus meant, and so that's not where I'm going. That's *Natural Revelation*. Everyone, even unbelievers, can look to these things and know there's a chance that a divine *Someone* is behind it.

I'm also not headed to where my confessional friends would expect, which is to the sacramental nature of the Lord's words, being that He said them within the context of the institution of the Lord's Supper. Yes, we see Him there, even as many can't or just won't. Still, that would be too easy, and that's not what started this thread spooling in my head, anyway.

I'm thinking of something else. I have Matthew 18:1-3 in mind.

Perhaps one of the best ways to figure out what I'm talking about is to set yourself at the feet of a Christian child. Wind the child up for discussion by mentioning Jesus, and then let him or her go. Let the little one do the instructing. Of course, not just any child can do this, but rather, one who is actually being raised in the faith—a little one who is taken to church with devout regularity, a child immersed in the discussions of faith at home with family, a child who'd consider it bizarre to eat a meal without first praying, whether at home or McDonald's. These kids can connect the dots far better than most adults.

I'll give you a very brief example.

This past Friday morning, my daughter Evelyn and I were making our way to school through the chilly darkness of a Michigan December. All the way there we listened and sang along to The Beach Boys.

California Girls. Good Vibrations. Fun, Fun, Fun. Surfin' Safari. Little Deuce Coupe. I Get Around. All of our favorites were gushing from the roll bar speakers of the Jeep.

Winter was upon us, and our hearts proved a longing for summer. But then, right in the middle of it...

"If summer were Christmas," Evelyn said, "these would be Advent songs."

"Wha—?"

I was stunned, and I nearly drove off the road. The ten-year-old girl was right. She could see a much bigger picture. She didn't have to search for Jesus. She was proving herself attuned to Him, showing it was far too natural for her to know Him by faith even at that very moment. In other words, she demonstrated her otherworldly eyesight by making the deeply intricate connection that Advent comes to us as people existing in the wintry darkness of sin and death. It sees us in our longing for rescue. And yet, it brings us along on hopeful melodies that look not only toward the warming sunrise of Jesus in Bethlehem, but to the full-on summer of His second coming at the Last Day.

Evelyn had connected the dots. She could see Jesus where the world could not. By her leading, I saw Him, too.

My prayer for you is that you would see Jesus so easily—that you would know He is with you in each and every moment.

I'll admit it can be a lot harder for adults in this regard. We're carrying things children aren't. Still, our Lord urges us to believe as they do, setting an even deeper plea before us: "Come to me, all you who are weary and burdened, and I will give you rest. Take my yoke upon you and learn from me, for I am gentle and humble in heart, and you will find rest for your souls. For my yoke is easy and my burden is light" (Matthew 11:28-30).

These are good words—just a few more dots in a design that sketches our kindly Advent King, Jesus.

✠

If Your Church Doesn't Worship on Christmas Day...

For a day in your courts is better than a thousand elsewhere. I would rather be a doorkeeper in the house of my God than dwell in the tents of wickedness. —Psalm 84:10

Ah, Christmas! The Feast of the Holy Nativity is upon us! That's right! The centuries-old celebration by the Christian Church that's spanned the globe and been considered by believers as an event of all events, second perhaps only to the Triduum—the holy "Three Days" of Maundy Thursday, Good Friday, and the Great Vigil of Easter—is just around the corner.

First, in the midst of this, most pastors are probably expecting Christmas Eve services to be well attended, but the actual festival day—the 25th—to be a bit thin. Speaking from experience, know your pastor is praying you'll make time for both days. In a sense, the 24th and 25th are a singular event.

In contrast to my words, I remember seeing an article a few years back from a fairly popular Christian author saying he was thankful to all the Christian churches that don't offer Christmas Day services. Being a pastor's kid, he was trying to say that he was glad the pastors of those churches would be able to dodge another exhausting (and based on the attendance numbers, often feels fruitless) effort to better use the time at home with the family like everyone else pretty much does.

Um. Okay.

Sure, I get what he thinks he's trying to say. I do. But he seems to have completely driven past the purpose for worship while saying it. In fact, at their root, his words make it sound as though it's actually possible for time with the Savior in worship to be considered a tiring inconvenience, that it has the potential for getting in the way of more important things like cooking and opening presents and time with family.

As concerned as his words might sound for the mental health of pastors, again, they sort of miss the mark of what Christian worship is all about, and not to mention why your pastor is doing what he's doing day in and day out in the first place. In fact, when it comes to enhancing your pastor's mental health, I dare say you might actually accomplish that by just showing up in church to receive the gifts of Christ he's been called to administer. I'm guessing that would make him smile, and it would probably lessen his inclination to whisper along with Isaiah, "O Lord, who has believed what he has heard from us? And to whom has the arm of the LORD been revealed?"

Even more, pastors, ask yourselves this: When it comes to holding the line for Christianity in a world ever increasing in its hostility toward you and the Christ you proclaim if the impression is given by the pastor that the most important celebrations of the year are negligible, what are you communicating concerning the every-Sunday gatherings?

Actually, let me just go ahead and be as clear as I can. What that "pastor's kid" author said was well-intended, but dumb. I get what he's saying namely because I know the situation intimately. But he's flat out wrong.

How about this instead? If your church has Christmas Eve services but doesn't offer a Christmas Day service, too—you know, the conjoined celebrations of the in-breaking of God into this world to conquer sin, death, and the devil—don't be glad for that. Instead, take a moment and consider what it means. And then after you've contemplated for a good thirteen seconds or so, call the church office and transfer your membership to a church that does offer a Christmas Day service, because right now, you're missing out.

Having gone ahead and crossed the proselytizing line, know that if you are ever in the neighborhood of Hartland, Michigan, look us up. The name is Our Savior Evangelical Lutheran Church and School. We're the tuition-free school on the north side of M-59 (Highland Road) just a little east of Fenton Road. No, not the ELCA church. That's west of Fenton Road. You're looking for the one east of Fenton Road. By the way, not only have I heard that it's a very friendly place, but I've heard worship means a lot to them. In fact, it means so much that they've never closed their doors for a scheduled worship service opportunity since they first opened back in 1955. Yeah, I know, right? Snowstorms? Whatever. Is the power out? They have candles. Did the furnace die? No biggie. Bundle up and sit more closely together!

In short, I hear they're pretty serious about what they do in that place. And why? Because they sure do like their time with Jesus.

✠

The Eve of the Nativity of Our Lord

Tonight is the Night

And she gave birth to her firstborn son and wrapped him in swaddling cloths and laid him in a manger, because there was no place for them in the inn. —Luke 2:7

Tonight is the night.

The whole concept of this night is beyond our ability to comprehend. There was an in-breaking between worlds. Yes, God is always with us. But tonight God became man.

Immanuel, God with us. Logos, the Word made flesh.

Tonight the divine Creator was born into human history as "us"—into the places we go, into the burdens of need that we own, into the whole of our existence. He became one of us to save all of us.

The in-breaking was signaled by an angel—a messenger—nine months before this night, as the timeline would go. The hymn joyfully embellishes, the angel came "with wings of drifted snow and eyes of flame." He spoke to a young, unmarried girl in Nazareth, a virgin. Calling her by name, he said, "Mary, you have found favor with God. You will bear a son. His name will be Jesus. He will be the Son of the Most High."

Luke's Gospel tells us that Mary was troubled by the visitation. And rightly so. The appearance of an angel means one of two things. It means either the promise of deliverance or a word of judgment ending in destruction. And so, as it must be when an angel has revealed his presence while bringing good news, "Don't be afraid," he speaks kindly. The in-breaking he reveals will not lead to our death, but rather will set into motion the final stages of the plan to win our salvation through the death and resurrection of the child conceived in her womb.

Her child is the answer to the sin problem.

Tonight is the night. It has finally happened. Angels have announced it, this time to the shepherds, telling them they needn't be frightened by this otherworldly visitation. Jesus has come. He's wrapped in swaddling clothes and lying in a manger. He's little. He has tiny fingers and toes. He has attentive eyes of love for His mother, Mary, and for His adoptive father, Joseph. He hears their voices when they sing hushed lullabies to Him in the crude feeding trough. He has begun as we began. And yet, He is Christ the Lord. He is the perfect in-breaking of God. This won't be visible to the human eyes in these first few moments. His birth was just as painfully messy as any birth before or after. The condition of His context: a manger—something far less than grand.

But still, He begins as we began, and yet, He is without sin. The in-breaking of the only One who can save us is finitely located here—right here as a sinless infant squirming in His lowly crib—opening and closing His eyes for the first time amidst the human experience, seeing and being all that it means to be us.

This little One will grow. He will live perfectly according to the Law. He will do the things that only God can do. He will raise the dead with a word, whispering into the ears of corpses and returning them to life. He will touch the lame and they will be in the right measure again. He will preach the Good News of forgiveness to all and the sorrowful hearts of His listeners will be restored.

He will lean into the ferocious headwinds of a world spinning into undoneness and He will turn it back on its axis.

A new axis will be anchored into the earth's frame. It will be a center post that makes everything right—tall and mounted at the top of Golgotha. The baby you see here in the manger, He will be the man pinned there. No matter where you've been or what you've done, His pain will win your freedom. No matter how long you've been away, His outstretched arms of suffering are a welcoming into His embrace of perfect love. His tears will wash away your sorrow. His cry, "It is finished!" will be the moment when the steely underpinnings in the frame of sin and death begin to groan, buckle, and collapse.

Tonight is the night.

"Fear not," the angels are repeating. Go and see. Go to the place where the Lord promises to be. Do as the others in your Christian family. Gather at the manger with the excitement of little ones overwhelmed by the joy of a newborn brother. Lift to your tiptoes. Peek between the shoulders and around the heads of your Christian siblings to get a glimpse of the One who is your redemption. He will be there. He'll be in the absolution spoken. He'll be in the preaching of the Christmas Gospel. He'll be in the Sacrament of His body and blood given and shed for you for the forgiveness of sins.

Tonight is the night. Don't miss it. Go to church. You'll certainly be welcomed. You'll most certainly be blessed because the divine One born in Bethlehem will be there.

In Him, you'll know the truest joy behind the words "Merry Christmas."

⊦

Not As Expected

He was in the world, and the world was made through him, yet the world did not know him. He came to his own, and his own people did not receive him. But to all who did receive him, who believed in his name, he gave the right to become children of God, who were born, not of blood nor of the will of the flesh nor of the will of man, but of God. And the Word became flesh and dwelt among us, and we have seen his glory, glory as of the only Son from the Father, full of grace and truth. —John 1:10-14

You know the story, yes?

It's the chronicle of a joyous event that resonated throughout the land, everyone in the kingdom rejoicing in celebration.

The word has gone out that under the plenty care of the kingdom's finest doctors and maids, the young mother, Mary, has given birth to a son, the heir.

We are swept away to the majestic palace high atop the hill, sturdied by brick and mortar, its towers rising high above the earth, adorned in smooth limestone carvings and gilded with gold trimmings, massive and mighty in posture against the horizon; the only proper and suitable location for the birth of the King of Kings, to be sure.

We are enjoined with our city—neighbors and kin, thousands upon thousand, as we pass through the ranks of legionnaires encamped near the city wall in tribute and honor, the rumbling of hooves and steeds clad in sterling armor. We travel past these regiments and through the grand arches of the forecourt gate, the palace walls lifting high, mounted and carefully guarded by parading soldiers looking down upon the crowd with readiness to keep order, men who will serve the will of this new King. We are carried along like a river to the palace door, being pressed on all sides by a populace excitedly awaiting with great hopefulness to get only a glimpse of the One who was born and will reign with Divine supremacy and strength.

Very few are privileged to press into and through the palace entrance. Only the clean, only those who are worthy, well-dressed, with unsoiled clothes and boots. Only the finest will be satisfactory. Each of these in the acceptable form is allowed in, pressing and taking eager positions within the vastness of the ornate vestibule swept clean with no traces of dust or filth, pauper or pest.

Looking up we see the partitioned ceilings soaring into the sky, painted with images and revealing chandeliers of fire and diamond gildings that glisten. The walls shout silently with colored flags and banners unfurled. The throne room hall is festooned for the new King.

The throne chancel before us is ready. In its apse, the minstrels are playing. The steps are sided by trumpeters in blazing red coats, prepared to sound the call of honor and prestige with fine-tuned blasts of exquisite harmony. The cathedrae for the joyous mother and father are stately and fine, indeed. Each seat is plush with purples and velvets. Solid gold and hammered silver form their frames. The cradle for the newborn child holds its place in the midst of these. It is wrapped in regalia, garnished with rubies and emeralds and sapphires, steadied by a marble mount that must be hoisted by more than a man. It is flanked by the muscular brawn of royal guards whose swords are drawn and at the ready for their infant charge.

A few, only the best, the finest, the privileged, most noble and respectable in the kingdom—the ones who have sought the King's favor by way of deed and treasure—only these are called forth by the court minister to visit and see.

But they are disappointed at their discovery. Behold, the cradle is empty, as are the cathedrae. The guardians of this King of Kings will not sit in these. The Son will not be found resting in this cradle.

This is not His story.

This was not God's plan.

I am hearing the prophet Isaiah's cadence drumming in my ears. His words describe the King's birth, and yet they are absurd to my senses. They speak of lowliness and suffering, and by such modesty, the sketch begins, the payment for sin is wrought and there is forgiveness, there is peace: "The virgin will conceive and give birth to a Son... The people walking in darkness have seen a great light; on those living in the land of the shadow of death and light has shined... For unto us a child is born, to us a son is given... He grew up before him like a tender shoot, and like a root out of the dry ground. He had no beauty or majesty to attract us to him, nothing in his appearance that we should desire Him. He was despised and rejected by men, a man of sorrows, and familiar with suffering... Surely He took up our infirmities and carried our sorrows, yet we considered Him stricken by God, smitten by him and afflicted. He was pierced for our transgressions, he was crushed for our iniquities; the punishment that brought us peace was upon Him, and by His wounds, we are healed."

I am hearing the strange tempo of the Apostle to the Gentiles, Paul, speaking with an astuteness sourced only by the power of the Holy Spirit: "God chose what is foolish in the world to shame the wise; God chose what is weak in the world to shame the strong; God chose what is low and despised in the world, even things that are not, to bring to nothing things that are, so that no human being might boast in the presence of God."

There is no boasting in oneself before this newborn King. There is no pride to be had in one's standing or one's merits or deeds before this Son who comes lowly, who takes a place lower than yourself. This King you seek is found in the filth of an animal stable. No legions surrounding to fortify. No palace walls or guard towers. No archways or chandeliers—only the blackened deep of the sky glittered with stars; only a dim lantern and its flame flickering in the gentle breeze, bobbing and bouncing, casting lonely shadows on kindling thin walls.

And far from her home, in the lineage town of her new husband, there's a young girl—not a queen, but a virgin. She is pushing and sweating and crying. She is wrestling against the tears and sorrow and agony of childbirth. No family comforting her. No skilled doctors to aid. No handmaidens to give care. Her husband, a carpenter, not a king with an entourage at his beckoning. He is clutching her hand through the hours and aiding as he can, caressing her face, fetching her water, and praying to *YaHWeH*, the God of His forefather, David, for comfort and peace and wisdom to care for this little One who has been revealed to him as the Savior of the world.

And in the fullness of time, in the bloody mess of human birth, amidst the less-than-royal court of cattle, sheep and such, in the cool evening sheltered by the rickety roof, so little to protect from this world's treachery, the child—Jesus—is born. He is the Son, the One whose Father is the eternal Creator. Here, the King of kings is born. Here He may be found. He was not heralded by royal riders scattered through the countryside to gather the masses in joy to make haste to greet Him.

But soon it will be that a king sends his horsemen to find Him and kill Him.

Soon it will be that we hear the thundering hooves stampeding the streets of Bethlehem and taking the lives of the innocent while a heavenly provision is made for the Lord's escape.

The Son came to that which was His own, but His own did not recognize Him. Here, in this throne room of humility, you will find Him. Trumpeted by angelic choirs to lowly, inadequate, undeserving, peasant shepherds who leave their flocks and travel across the plains of Bethlehem to discover their salvation. The first to visit and view Him—sweaty, sandals dirty, dirty fingernails, the animal stench, hands soiled from the grime of their trade—they kneel at the splintery manger in humility and faith and gaze into the eyes of this infant, hastily wiped clean and wrapped in swaddling clothes by an adoptive and nervous father, lowly and resting in a bed of hay. This is the sign they were given by the angel. And so they are now the first participants in that first, great Divine Service of worshipers who see and receive the incarnate God. These lowly, undeserving sinners hear and believe this Gospel of forgiveness and peace first preached by the angels, and they know without fear, they are beholding God in the flesh. And so they leave that grand and beautiful cathedral—the little stable—and they live and they breathe and they shout the message to all they find, only to return once more to the fields renewed.

This, now, is the story. It is your story.

It is this story that begins at Christmas and gives to you life.

It is this Gospel that rings out across the world at Christmas in celebration of God's great glory, wrapped up and seated in the wonderfully less-than-spectacular and scandalous event of Christmas.

Behold the King of Kings and the Lord of Lords, Jesus Christ. He is the lowly King who is born this day to serve you and bring to you peace with God. He is the sinless Son who will withstand the temptations of the devil. He is the worker of great miracles. He will give sight to the blind and legs to the lame. He will raise the dead to life. He is the faithful preacher of the Gospel, the One who receives sinners, forgives them, and makes them new. He is the innocent lamb led before the Sanhedrin and Pilate, the lamb led to His slaughter. He is the gracious Savior who gives Himself over fully to death on a cross to accomplish what we in the filthiness of our sin could not. He is the valiant victor who casts the stone door away from the tomb and breaks forth from the shackles of death with great might, bearing the scars which declare that the veil of sin which covers this world in darkness has been lifted. He is the One who ascends into heaven and sits at the right hand of the Father to rule over the land, and sea, and air, and cosmos; all things within His domain.

May God grant to you the faith to bend your knee at the crude cradle of Jesus. May you do it with a sure and certain hope that this child, born of Mary, was born for you.

O, come let us adore Him, *Christ*, the *Lord*!

✝

What's Next

Seek the Lord and his strength; seek his presence continually! Remember the wondrous works that he has done, his miracles and the judgments he uttered. —1 Chronicles 16:11-12

C an you believe it's New Year's Eve? I sure can't. The days from this past year seem to have flown by.

I wonder what the Lord has in store for the coming year. I know one thing He's planning: His gifts of forgiveness for you through the ministry of Word and Sacrament. That never changes. And that's good because we need Him to be consistent, predictable, steady, and sure. Why? Because we aren't. And neither is the world in which we live.

Sure, the sun keeps rising and shining, the seasons keep changing so predictably, and the whole world seems to be about its regular business. But remember, the Lord is the One maintaining these things. The fabric of the world—all that comprises its nature—has been corrupted by sin. With this, it is both unsteady and untrustworthy. The world and its mammonous things will fail us.

But God won't.

The next time you have doubts about this, take a quick look at a crucifix. You might not feel anything in particular, but you'll see something. You'll see in the image a hint as to God's current and future plans for you because of the giving of His Son for your salvation. You may even be reminded that while sometimes everything else was, and is even now, very unsure—even our own selves—God acted on our behalf. Jesus, Bethlehem's infant champion, set His face like flint to the edge and then into utter

31

darkness from which no one could ever emerge. His death beamed brightly in that blackness. It shattered the unsteady swirls and the unreliable messes that we not only make for ourselves, but those that we endure at the hands of the unholy trinity: the Devil, the World, and the Sinful Flesh.

My prayer for you is that you have been reinvigorated by the Christmas festival just celebrated, that you have been made keen to behold the light of Christ each and every day and that you will continue to look for and expect the simple and mundane, but powerfully saving gifts God gives with such regularity day in and day out throughout the entirety of the year. Word and Sacrament are where it's at, my friends—Absolution, the preaching of the Gospel, the Lord's Supper, Holy Baptism—all God's Word given in wonderfully tangible ways.

The New Year is sure to be a medley of completely different challenges, but thanks be to God that our Lord will never let up with all that's required for navigating into the safe harbors of His wonderful grace.

✠

In That Hour, Pray

Rejoice always, pray without ceasing, give thanks in all circumstances; for this is the will of God in Christ Jesus for you. —1 Thessalonians 5:16-18

A happy New Year to you and blessings!

So, did you make any resolutions for the New Year? I did, and by God's grace, I hope to keep them. Making life changes, especially when it feels like the changes go against the basic grains of one's character, is really hard. Even the Lord acknowledged this to the disciples in the Garden of Gethsemane when He said, "The spirit is willing, but the flesh is weak," and so in that same instance, the Lord urges us to pray for the strength of spirit to overcome the desires of the flesh.

Prayer.

How often do you pray? And I'm not so sure the slip-up on the icy patch of the freeway where you repeated His name over and over again actually counts. Although, I wasn't there, so I don't know for sure. Either way, the question still stands: How often do you pray?

I can say that I pray relatively often. You should expect that of your pastor, to be sure. I'll add that I've been praying a lot more than usual these days, especially at the bedside of people living through special circumstances that call for the prayers of others. Pastor Jakob Heckert is one of those people. I pray there with him often. Almost daily, in fact.

But before I share more about that, let me get back to my original question one more time. How often do you pray? I hope it's an everyday thing for you—or at least that it's often. If you don't, I don't mean to make you feel guilty about it, however, I sure would suggest that you're missing out on the opportunity to participate in the wonderfully free gift of speaking to the One who, as Isaiah said, made the entire cosmos, the One who made the stars and calls them all by name. The Creator of the world loves you, and He has opened Himself up to us in Jesus Christ in a way that allows us complete and total access to His throne of grace with any and all requests. And ultimately, this has no lesser result than that He hears us, and He responds to the petition with that which will serve for our eternal life in Jesus.

For those of you who do pray fairly regularly, I'll bet you have those times and places where it happens the most. For all others, I would suggest the same. Think of a place where you find yourself almost every day—whether it is in the car driving to work, before meals or bedtime, or any other time or place that you can think of— and make it a priority to speak with your God. If you don't know what to say, I recommend you grab a Lutheran Service Book and open up to page 305 ("Prayers, Intercessions, and Thanksgivings"). There are plenty of prayers from which to choose. Or you could pray the best prayer that was ever written: The Lord's Prayer. Christ gave us that prayer for a reason, in one sense, because it is both centrifugal and centripetal in nature—that is, it concerns itself with others around us while at the same time speaking to each concern that we meet. That's pretty great, I think.

And while I'm on the subject, if you need help with devotional materials, ask your pastor. I'm sure he can send you in the right direction for acquiring something edifying. Perhaps that could be your New Year's resolution.

Anyway, I just got back from Pastor Heckert's home a few moments ago, and you should know that the end of his earthly journey is not far away. Still, even though his eyes have grown much dimmer and he struggles to speak, his line of sight to Christ is unhindered and his voice is confident. His last words to me today before he fell asleep were, first, that he loved me. I, of course, told him I loved him, too, because I do. It will be very hard to say goodbye when the hour comes. But then he said rather softly that he has no doubt, that he has certainty in the face of death. Then he went on to confess his faith several times—almost creedally—saying over and over that he believed in the Triune God—Father, Son, and Holy Spirit—and that he believed that Jesus Christ is the only way of salvation. And then he asked me to help him pray to this same God who loves him and was listening to his words. And so I did. We prayed several Psalms, the Lord's Prayer, I prayed several spontaneous prayers, and then it was Pastor Heckert who brought it to a conclusion, and I think because he was having difficulty staying awake. Essentially, he said that he knew he had lived, that he would die, but that in Christ he would never die. He said one more time that he has no doubt in this regard.

And then he fell asleep.

Imagine if God was closed off to us in such an hour.

But he isn't. Go to Him. Speak to Him often. Even better, be present in worship where He gives the gifts of His forgiveness for the strengthening of a faith that knows without a doubt that His love is preserving and He will never let you go—not even at the hour of death. Don't starve yourself of such confidence. Don't neglect the right you've been given to approach God—to call Him "Father" and to know that you are His dear child.

Pray. He is listening. As His baptized child, you will always be someone for whom He has a care.

☩

The First Sunday after Christmas

You Belong Here

One thing have I asked of the Lord, that will I seek after: that I may dwell in the house of the Lord all the days of my life. —Psalm 27:4

I pray all is well and that the Lord is blessing your New Year with the peace of Christ.

Admittedly, and obviously, as the pastor of a congregation, I have a very different perspective than most when it comes to the Lord's house. Now, I don't mean that it's better. I mean it's different. For example, the view from the altar, pulpit, and lectern is very different than the view from the pews or the choir loft. Here's another example. This one is a bit stranger.

Over the course of the last few years, we endured some pretty ferocious weather in Michigan. That being said, there were four or five Saturday nights when I found it necessary to sleep at the church to assure that the lights would be on and the doors would be open for Sunday worship the very next day. The pastor before me made it a point that if a Divine Service was scheduled, it was going to happen, and the only thing that would be cause for canceling would be the Lord's return in glory. I agree, and so I have no intention of ever letting a cancellation happen on my watch. But the problem is that I live considerably further away from the church than my predecessor, and so with that, a sleepover is necessary.

Nevertheless, the point of this little narrative is to say that at 2 AM, when the lights are out and the snow is crackling against the windows, when the howling winds are creeping in and echoing through the empty halls, the church building becomes a very different place—almost alien. When it's empty and dark and the voices of the day have all gone, this place is only half itself. Its guts are gone and you can feel it.

But when it's bright and full—when the children are giggling in the school classrooms and corridors, when the worshippers are gathering together to sing their full-throated praises, when the sermon is booming and the organ is rattling the soldered seams of the stained glass, when the study-goers are calling out in discussion and the whole group is learning and laughing together—this place becomes otherworldly in a different sense, almost heavenly. It becomes the fullness of its identity when its innards—you, the body of believers—return. And in this return, the Lord proves Himself to be at work by His Holy Spirit gathering His people to a place where He can be with them, where eternal life will beam because the gift of forgiveness through Word and Sacrament is being doled out with such plenty that you'd never think these hallways could ever be dark or that there could ever be silence in the rafters.

In the end, this place is what it is because of Christ and not us. And yet, Christ gathers people. And it is into people that Christ places His mercy—the light and life of His love—so that when the building's rooms are dark and the noise is much less, we know that the true light hasn't been extinguished. It's simply gone out with those to whom God has given it (Matthew 5:14).

With that, know that you belong here. When you're gone, you're missed. Your light is a big deal to your pastor and the rest of your Christian family. This is certainly something I ponder while lying on the cot in my office in the middle of a blustery winter's night.

Up and Doing

All Scripture is breathed out by God and profitable for teaching, for reproof, for correction, and for training in righteousness. —2 Timothy 3:16

So, have you made any resolutions for the New Year? I have. This year I'll be giving extra effort to rebuilding broken relationships in my life. I want to do what I can to fix the fractures.

We'll see how it goes. Only God knows what'll happen in such circumstances. I just know I want to try to give it more attention, maybe be more deliberate in reaching out.

Making New Year's resolutions gets a bad rap. It was F.M. Knowles who said, "He who breaks a resolution is a weakling. He who makes one is a fool." I disagree. I don't think it's foolish. In fact, if you don't already make resolutions, I'd encourage you to give it a try. You'd be amazed at how making resolutions helps bring focus to other parts of life. It helps to identify a destination of betterment and then to aim for it, even if only to get closer. That's not a bad thing. From a biblical perspective, it can be considered "training in righteousness" (2 Timothy 3:16). In that sense, I suppose rather than being a fan of Knowles, I'm more of a Henry Wadsworth Longfellow kind of guy. Observing life, and in one sense, simply desiring to go about living in a way that tries to move goodness forward, Longfellow said, "Let us then be up and doing, with a heart for any fate; still achieving, still pursuing, learn to labor and to wait."

I like that.

From the vantage point of Christianity, to be up and doing with a heart for any fate—learning to labor and to wait—certainly has resonating potential. We're active in the world around us. We're up and doing in ways that reveal a pursuing of faithfulness to Christ. With that, we learn to labor at certain times and we learn to wait during others. This is trust. And in the end, come what may—any fate, any and all results—we're already comfortable with the fact that these are God's to determine. We hold to the simple conviction that He will work for the good of those who love Him, and He will use our efforts (which are empowered by the Holy Spirit), even what we believe to be our extreme inabilities, to be a light to others to see His glory.

I like that, too.

And so I've made some resolutions. I told you one. I have another one, but I'll keep that one to myself. Either way, with both I want to be *up and doing* to accomplish something beyond myself for others, and as I do this, my prayer is that I'll be ready for any fate in every situation. I trust that God will handle the results. I just want to be faithful.

If you decide to do the same in the New Year, I pray that the Lord will bless you in your efforts. Know that I'll be rooting for you. And know that if you don't fully accomplish whatever it is you're setting out to accomplish—at least not as you might interpret the word "accomplish"—by the power of the Holy Spirit at work in you for eyes set on Christ and a heart seeking faithfulness to Him, rest assured that God will use you to move His love a little further along in a world in such desperate need of receiving it. I guarantee this will happen even if you never see it.

☩

EPIPHANY

Twenty Enter, Nineteen Leave

Jesus said to her, "I am the resurrection and the life. Whoever believes in me, though he die, yet shall he live." —John 11:25

Although it's often very hard to navigate the swirling tempest of worldly reason, I know by faith, just as Job knew, that even though my flesh will return to the dust, I will stand before the Lord and see Him with my own eyes. I know all believers will rise again in the flesh and we will be together in the glories of heaven for all eternity.

Now, let me put this into the perspective I experienced before departing for the grave-side service of a dear colleague and friend.

After the funeral luncheon, I made my way back to my office where I put some things away and then made some preparations for the Sunday morning Divine Service that would be occurring the very next day. Knowing I had about five minutes before I needed to leave to get to the cemetery on time, I sat down and rendered some thoughts by way of a social media post. Here's what I wrote.

> We'll be leaving in a few moments to put into the bosom of the earth the mortal remains of our dear friend and pastor, Jakob K. Heckert. The words of the Creed regarding our Savior, Jesus, ring in our ears: "…was crucified, died, and was buried."
>
> Buried. Considering the events of death, the stinger at the tip of this word carries a very unique venom.
>
> Of course, Jakob is in heaven, but in a very human sense, until the cemetery, he was with us. There he was in his bed at home. There he was in the casket at the funeral home. There he was in the casket in the narthex. Even though the lid was closed, there he was beneath it and under the pall during the Divine Service. There he was in the

back of the coach. There he was for any of us at any moment to reach out and touch.

There he was.

But now twenty of us will enter the cemetery and only nineteen will leave. We will be less one person, one friend.

In such a moment, the words from the Creed just beyond those describing the Lord's victorious death and consequent burial are so desperately needed: "He descended into hell. The third day He rose again from the dead."

Resurrection. Ponder this.

"I am the resurrection and the life," Jesus said. "He who believes in Me will live, even though he dies; and whoever lives and believes in Me will never die." Twenty believers enter the cemetery sturdied by the Gospel for faith. Twenty believers traverse a muddy landscape pocked with headstones, and they go knowing that even if any or all must remain behind, all twenty will rise again.

That's the anti-venom of promise to be given in the moment. It's the medicine that disarms the sting.

These words are a reflection of the wrestling between the sinner and the saint—the sinner seeing a somber gathering of people in a place full of dead bodies, and the saint seeing that which the Holy Spirit has worked in believers, which is full trust in the promise and eventual reality of the resurrection of all flesh as it has been won by the life, death, and resurrection of Jesus Christ, the Son of God, our Savior.

With that, there's a reason we say the Christian creeds each and every Sunday. The words of such a Gospel confession are important enough that they must be ever at the edge of our hearts and minds, as well as resting at the tip of our tongues. We need a clear confession of the Christian faith when the fog of reason is threatening to overcome us.

It sure did threaten me on Saturday. But I'm confident that the Holy Spirit worked within me trust in the promise to know that even in such moments, Christ holds onto me with both hands, and He will never leave nor forsake me. He intends that I would look upon death—the formidable foe that it is—and see a toothless, clawless, and defeated specter; one that has no hold on me. And if this is true, then the graves of the faithful are little more than beds in the earth that keep our remains until our God says the word, the angels move into place, the trumpet sounds and the souls of God's people in heaven are reunited to their resurrected bodies—now perfected— and we are ushered before the throne in the flesh.

That's the endpoint for the buried body of a Christian—eternity in heaven, and not the ground.

I pray this same comfort and knowledge for you. It certainly is yours as much as it is mine.

✠

Beyond "Therefore"

I appeal to you therefore, brothers, by the mercies of God, to present your bodies as a living sacrifice, holy and acceptable to God, which is your spiritual worship. —Romans 12:1

I suppose there's a chance that you have a day off from work in celebration of the national holiday remembering Martin Luther King, Jr. It certainly is a worthwhile day of remembrance honoring a man of diligent service to humanity. He accomplished much, and he did so in a way that was shocking to his enemies.

When they threatened him with violence and death, even the death of his wife and children, he spoke to peace.

Interestingly, while Martin Luther King, Jr. didn't necessarily align with the Lutheran theologies that would have put us in altar fellowship, his theological understandings of what to do amid persecution and his fundamental thoughts on being a slave to Christ as opposed to a slave to man should leave most of us in awe. He got those things so incredibly right, and for that, he is to be wholeheartedly appreciated.

I preached rather recently on the text of Romans 12:6-16. During the sermon, I mentioned that quite a bit hinges on Paul's usage of the word "therefore." It was noted that the word wasn't in the actual reading, but had we gone back and collected Paul's thoughts from the beginning of the chapter (as well as other chapters), we would've heard it, and we would have been situated to see that the long list of do's and do-not's in chapter 12 isn't necessarily an exhortation, but rather a description.

The texts that come before the "therefore" speak of God's mercy to us. This teaches us that what follows the "therefore" is not a list of demands, but rather a portrait of who we are because of what Christ has done for us and works through us by His grace.

By the power of the Holy Spirit, God creates a different kind of person, a person who fits the description and is capable of seeing himself as one who is no longer in bondage to the world, but rather serves Christ and is capable of doing so in ways that simply flabbergast the world around us.

We are made into those who can be hopeful during struggle. We can pray for our persecutors. We can love our enemies. We can confound the world in these ways, and in so doing, we are found to be lights of Christ leading others to Him even amid sin's darkness.

If anything, Dr. King understood these things, and I appreciate his unbending fervor for living it out and being a real, tangible, national icon of this biblical truth. It certainly would seem that his cause is being lost on so many, nevertheless, history's record unarguably stands in favor of a man who sought faithfulness to Christ in his effort to rid the world of the tarry and vile tendency to see others according to the color of their skin and not the content of their character.

Few come along with a willingness to do what he did. Maybe it's because few are called to do so with such courage in a public way. Nevertheless, each of us has been recreated to be God's people in the simplicity and normalcy of our daily vocations. This, too, takes courage, and in the end, is never to be considered small. In fact, it's really quite grand. It's grand because of the gravity God attaches to it. It's in these daily interactions that others behold the Gospel of Christ at work in a real person, and by this, onlookers are affected in a Gospel way (Matthew 5:13-16). Their attention is turned to God. They are found curious, thoughtful, concerned, questioning—interested. And God worked this out by you just being you.

May God bless your day and week as you stand in His grace and beam this mighty and courageous love to the world around you. I know he will. I do not doubt that Romans 12 will be a description of you.

✝

A Child in Prayer

Therefore, my beloved brothers, be steadfast, immovable, always abounding in the work of the Lord, knowing that in the Lord your labor is not in vain. —1 Corinthians 15:58

Here in my Christian day school, I call upon the eighth-grade boys to serve as lectors during the chapel services. This means that sometime between arriving at school and the beginning of the Matins service at 8:10 AM, the one on duty for that day makes his way down to church nave, gets vested, and then looks over the Epistle reading appointed for the upcoming Sunday. And then during the service, he reads it to the children.

I can say that throughout the year, the young men have grown much more comfortable in the effort and are doing a splendid job. But simply to report this is not why I am sharing the account. I want to share something a little more inspiring—something that serves as a reassurance to all of us that our Christian Day School is worth every bit of toil and tears we've put into it over the years.

When I walked into the nave to set the lectern and lectionary in place for the service (which I usually try to do long before anyone else is in there), the student for the day was already there, vested, and kneeling at the altar rail praying. I, of course, did not do what I'd gone into the nave to do until he was done. I didn't want to disturb him.

But there he knelt in the vastness of an empty nave—the candles aglow beyond him, the windows darkened by the early morning snow—and he prayed silently. One of God's little ones was acting on God's promise that he had complete access to His Savior, offering petitions from his heart that he had, at that moment, been moved to speak.

If I could've taken a photo, I would've. It was an instant reminder that we aren't just trying to educate children according to the typical philosophies; that is, we aren't just trying to create workers who have skills and personal styles to fill and perform jobs, or to develop active citizens who recognize their own capacity for personal achievement and contribute to the society. Of course, we try at these things, but in the end, we have a much more important goal behind our efforts. Everything we attempt to do arises from the objective truth of the Gospel—the Good News of the forgiveness of sins through the life, death, and resurrection of Jesus Christ. With that as our constant heading—our north star of calibration—we are really striving toward a better thing, which in my opinion, Luther defined pretty well when he took a moment to comment on the goals of Christian education. He said so simply that the job of a Christian school is to bring children "to believe, to live, to pray, to suffer, and to die."

In any school, there are struggles and there are successes. I just witnessed one of the fruits of success, and for that, I am humbly thankful to God that Christian education exists and that it continues to move forward supported by people who have been moved by the Gospel and are just as thankful.

In conclusion, consider this little story for all that it is: a Gospel-driven encouragement to "be steadfast, immovable, always abounding in the work of the Lord, knowing that in the Lord your labor is not in vain"!

☩

Cue the Bolt of Lightning

Commit your way to the LORD; trust in him, and he will act. —Psalm 37:5

I think it was Luther who said something about how Man has a difficult time knowing his own sin, and that more often he believes his blindness to be his highest wisdom.

That's insightful. In fact, it reminds me of the warning God gives to His priests in Hosea 4:4, 6:

> For with you is my contention, O priest... My people are destroyed for lack of knowledge...

The point: Without God's help, without God revealing to Man in some way that he is doing wrong, Man will likely continue to move along in the ignorance of his sin, perhaps even considering his own efforts, all things he does with the best of intentions—things he does for the benefit of family, for self, for work, for life in general—as being wise, when in reality it is harmful to the soul and dreadfully diminishing of his relationship with Christ.

I share this as I consider the events of this past Sunday. My congregation welcomed one of my former seminary professors as a guest preacher and teacher. At one point on Saturday evening while he and I were sitting together and visiting over a couple of my nicer whiskies, after my wife, Jennifer, had gone upstairs to tuck the kids into bed, he asked about attendance numbers and the basic demographics of the congregation. I shared some of the details— about how things are really turning around in this place in some pretty amazing ways. But somehow during the conversation, I was drawn to confess to him a very personal frustration: Many of our families with young children appear to care so much more about making sure their kids are involved in sports—hockey, wrestling, or whatever—rather than being in worship and Bible study. Confirmation responsibilities on Sunday morning? Sure, when hockey season is done. Worship and Sunday School? No, not this week or next. We have indoor soccer tournaments that will consume the next two weekends completely.

Not all, but unfortunately, far too many families are caught up in this swirling torrent of making sure that our children are socially adaptable or well-rounded individuals, seemingly unaware as to just how harmful it is, that by doing this we are actually training them to see time with Jesus as optional—and for that matter, that the time with the Lord isn't even the most preferred option among the ones vying for our attention. All of this is pretty much an unabashed casting aside of the First and Third Commandments, as well as the duties of parents well-established by the Fourth Commandment. It doesn't even seem to blush as it shuns all of the New Testament texts which mandate togetherness with Christ and His Church for the benefit of our souls as He feeds us through Word and Sacrament.

I dare say, the attention given to these other priorities is the reason we saw our attendance drop to nearly two-thirds of its normal number this past Sunday. But in the end, I suppose what bothers me more than anything else is the fact that we continue to do this deliberately. Christian parents are starving and killing the souls of an entire generation of children. And they think they are doing the right thing.

Cue the lightning bolt.

So, what did the good professor say to me this past Saturday night about this?

"You're the pastor, Thoma," he said in a round-about way. "What have you done to show these people their sins?"

Hmm. What have I done? I guess I sort of preach about it here and there. I touch on the topic in Bible study occasionally. But again, if people aren't in regular attendance in these places, they will have missed it. Have I steered into it directly? Have I ever thought about dedicating an entire newsletter to the issue? Have I come right out and given the knowledge of the Scriptures to God's people? Perhaps not.

For with you is my contention, O priest. My people are destroyed for lack of knowledge.

People of God, forgive your pastors for failing you in this way, whether it was for fear of offending you, or because of a level of apathy. Hear now the Word of the Lord's lawful warning as it meets this challenge among the gathered saints in the churches.

Worship and Bible study are not optional.

Don't ever fool yourself into thinking that it is. There's only one other character outside of you with such a scheming intention: the Devil. He does not want you in worship (or study) because he knows that it is of the utmost essential for your life and faith and it is where you belong. And so, when you begin to consider it as just another gathering of like-minded people—a country club measure of sights and sounds that you can take or leave—behold as the writer to the Hebrews (chapter 12) pulls back the spiritual curtain on holy worship and warns:

> For you have not come to what may be touched, a blazing fire and darkness and gloom and a tempest and the sound of a trumpet and a voice whose words made the hearers beg that no further messages be spoken to them… But you have come to Mount Zion and to the city of the living God, the heavenly Jerusalem, and to innumerable angels in festal gathering, and to the assembly of the firstborn who are enrolled in heaven, and to God, the judge of all, and to the spirits of the righteous made perfect, and to Jesus, the mediator of a new covenant, and to the sprinkled blood that speaks a better word than the blood of Abel. See that you do not refuse him who is speaking.

> For if they did not escape when they refused him who warned them on earth, much less will we escape if we reject him who warns from heaven... Therefore let us be grateful for receiving a kingdom that cannot be shaken, and thus let us offer to God acceptable worship, with reverence and awe, for our God is a consuming fire.

With this in mind, step back in the same inspired Word to chapter 11, which speaks not only to the confidence of our baptismal right as Christians to be with God in worship, but to be careful not to refuse those who warn us when we fall away to other distractions, or even worse, when we set our hearts and minds upon other things and deliberately refuse Christ as He comes to be with us, most especially by the preaching and the Lord's Supper:

> Therefore, brothers, since we have confidence to enter the holy places by the blood of Jesus, by the new and living way that he opened for us through the curtain, that is, through his flesh, and since we have a great priest over the house of God, let us draw near with a true heart in full assurance of faith, with our hearts sprinkled clean from an evil conscience and our bodies washed with pure water. Let us hold fast the confession of our hope without wavering, for he who promised is faithful. And let us consider how to stir up one another to love and good works, not neglecting to meet together, as is the habit of some, but encouraging one another, and all the more as you see the Day drawing near. For if we go on sinning deliberately after receiving the knowledge of the truth, there no longer remains a sacrifice for sins, but a fearful expectation of judgment, and a fury of fire that will consume the adversaries. Anyone who has set aside the Law of Moses dies without mercy on the evidence of two or three witnesses. How much worse punishment, do you think, will be deserved by the one who has spurned the Son of God, and has profaned the blood of the covenant by which he was sanctified, and has outraged the Spirit of grace?

I know. These are tough words to hear. And not just because they speak to some, but because they speak to all of us. Every one of us is guilty of such spiritual recklessness. Even me. Again, please forgive me.

Now hear the Word of the Gospel—and I will most certainly be listening to it for myself as I write it.

God knows the heart of sinful Man. He knows the innermost desire to absent ourselves from His presence. He knows it well because it was the very first thing Mankind did in the Garden after the fall into sin. We hid from Him. But God did not leave us there. His first words to fallen Man were to seek and find him. "Where are you?" He called to Adam—to us. This tells you a lot about your God. He loves you. He does not give up on you. He does not want to lose you. He does not want to lose your children.

In Jesus Christ, He has reached out to all of us in the fullest of ways. He took upon Himself human flesh and gave up His life to redeem us—to buy us back from sin, death, and the power of the Devil. In our baptism, He has poured upon us the merits of this work and He has recreated us to be His children—little ones of faith who see the world and all of its trappings around us in a very different way; to have priorities that are no longer as that of the world. How can this be? Because we are forgiven. We are holy. The Holy Spirit lives in us as God's people. We are no longer as we were before.

Thanks be to God for this!

Now, repent. The Gospel gives all that is necessary for amending the sinful life. Repent and change. Don't be mad. Don't get angry and begin seeking out a church that keeps silent on these things, one that is unwilling to steer into this with you for fear of offending you. You don't want that. The Lord's Word already told you that you don't need that. You need truth. Rejoice now that the one God has set in place to give this to you has indeed given it. Why? Because it changes the results of God's own dreadful foretelling: *"My people are destroyed for lack of knowledge."*

Your pastor doesn't want this for you.

Now, before closing, I should make a quick clarification. If you are planning to be away for a tournament, no problem. Just be sure to find a faithful congregation and go to church. I know for a fact that some of our families do this, and for that, I commend their faithfulness. Either way, just know that you don't have to be here, but you do need to be in worship. That's the priority. Be fed. Don't skip it and think you'll pick it up next week. Habits form and it becomes all too easy to slip away.

And so, with all of this being said, know that I'm praying for you. Know that I am trusting that by the Gospel truth that has been given, God—the Father, the Son, and the Holy Spirit—will strengthen you, and He will bless and preserve you as His holy child.

I won't stop moving with this important kind of encouragement. You need it. I need it. We all need the rightly divided Law and Gospel. Thanks be to God that our Lord has given these to us as the treasures that they are!

☩

Full of Goodness

Now you are the body of Christ and individually members of it.
—1 Corinthians 12:27

Saint Paul wrote something rather interesting in Romans 15. Here's what he said:

> I myself am convinced, my brothers, that you yourselves are full of goodness, complete in knowledge and competent to instruct one another (v.14).

What did he mean by this?

Well, first he meant what it sounds like he meant—that by the power of the Spirit at work through the Gospel in each of them, they were full of goodness—and this means that even while they wrestled with the sinful nature each and every day, through faith in Jesus they could produce the fruits of faith made ready by the Gospel. We know what those fruits are since Paul already told us that the fruits of the Spirit are peace, patience, kindness, goodness, etc. These particular fruits produce thoughts, words, and deeds in the world around us that emanate in a variety of ways.

The second thing he meant, at least partially, is that we are gathered together as a fellowship that knows these things and are fully competent for encouraging one another and building one another up according to faith in Jesus.

We need one another. We need each member to work together—to take the gifts of knowledge and skill God has seen fit to give and to share them where appropriate throughout the Church. If you are a carpenter, ask how you might put those skills to use. If you are a skilled seamstress, let us know. We have vestments that could use your help. Are you wise with finances? Teach us how to reach out within the fellowship to gauge our directions and make sturdier, long-term plans.

As a believer, by God's grace, you are full of goodness. This is an uplifting truth, and for that I am grateful.

If There Were No Christians

But in your hearts honor Christ the Lord as holy, always being prepared to make a defense to anyone who asks you for a reason for the hope that is in you; yet do it with gentleness and respect. —1 Peter 3:15

I came across a rather straight-shooting, and yet uplifting, portion of commentary from Martin Luther during my own time of devotional study. The text from the Bible that he was considering was from 2 Corinthians 6:10, which reads in part: "…as poor, yet making many rich; as having nothing, and yet possessing all things." Here's what Luther said about this:

> If there were no Christians on earth, no town or land would have peace, yes, in one single day the devil would ruin everything there is on earth. The fact that there is still corn growing in the fields, that men recover from their illnesses, that they have food, peace, and security, all this they owe to the Christians. Indeed, we are poor beggars, and yet we make many rich. In very truth, we possess nothing, and yet we have all things; and whatever kings, princes, citizens, and peasants have in this world, they have it, not because of their fair hair, but because of Christ and His Christians. To them is given the Gospel, Baptism, and the Sacrament to convert the people, to win souls from the devil, to snatch them out of hell and death, and take them to heaven; and again to strengthen, comfort, and uphold the poor and instruct and advise the afflicted consciences in their sore temptation; and again to teach all people in all occupations how to do their work as good Christians. This sort of work kings and emperors, the mighty and the rich, the learned and the wise cannot perform, nor could they pay for it with all their possessions. For there is not one amongst them who could comfort and cheer a single soul when it is burdened and weighed down by sin. (W.A. 45. 532)

That's great, isn't it? Powerful, too. Luther reminds us that the effort of the Christian Church is never in vain as it works to bring the Gospel into a world in need. The Gospel is to be at the heart of every church's efforts. It's by the Gospel that people are converted and souls are snatched away from Satan, death, and hell.

Whether you realize it or not, your church is on the front lines of this effort, which means, as a Christian, you are, too. And as you read from Luther, without the Christians carrying this Gospel forth, there would be nothing left to remove the burden of sin from the shoulders of a world in need.

This is how the Lord has structured it, and you are a part. By the power of the Holy Spirit, take heart and be courageous in your calling to speak the hope that is within you as each opportunity arises. As you do this, invite your listeners to your church. Bring them to the place designated by Christ for administering the thirst-quenching peace of His mercy to the parched inhabitants of this fallen world.

✟

A Christian Leader

Blessed is the man who walks not in the counsel of the wicked, nor stands in the way of sinners, nor sits in the seat of scoffers. —Psalm 1:1

I saw the sun this past weekend! I love the sun! Did you see it, too? I was pretty excited by it, that's for sure. I've read about the sun in books, but living here in Michigan, I've rarely caught a glimpse of it. It sure made my day to see this cosmic phenomenon that others talk about so fondly. I even saw a sunbeam on dry pavement. Dry pavement! Can you believe that?! It didn't have any snow on it!

Okay, so I'm being a little facetious. The point is that the warmer weather has finally poked through the pall of a long Michigan winter, and with that, some relief is upon us.

Besides a big and brightly-beaming sun casting its happy light upon us, do you know what else I love? The leaders in my congregation. And why? Because they truly do fit the Biblical depiction of what it means to emanate Godly authority in the Church. In other words, they see themselves as both responsible and accountable.

Concerning accountability, the Word of God is pretty clear that anyone serving in a sphere of authority over others will ultimately give an account to the One who is the source of all authority (Luke12:42-48; 20:9-16). And we know who that is, right? Read Matthew 28:18 if you don't. But if you guessed Jesus before reading Mathew 28, then give yourself a high five, because you're right. All authority in heaven and on earth is His, and so even the authority that leaders in the Church and world wield, they do so as stewards of Christ.

Concerning responsibility, believe it or not, the Scriptures suggest that Godly character is essential for anyone seeking to be a leader. Maybe you have heard the phrase "Character is your true self when no one is watching." In the Bible, the traits of Godly character are almost always intimately paired with "truth." Even more interestingly, character is treated as a fruit born from conviction, which is at the heart of the positions we take concerning truth. A leader with character seeks after truth—God's truth—and wants it to be communicated to the people he or she is leading (Proverbs 6:16-19; Psalm 1:1; 1 Corinthians 11:1-2; Romans 5:4; 1 John 2:3-4; John 6:67-71; Proverbs 22:1; Proverbs 8:14; 2 Thessalonians 2:14-15; James 4:8; Ecclesiastes 7:1; Philippians 4:5; Ephesians 5:1; 2 Corinthians 5:17).

In Titus 2:15, Saint Paul takes time to point out how a Christian leader's authority is founded on character. Paul encourages:

> Declare these things; exhort and rebuke with all authority. Let no one disregard you.

Now, Paul does not mean that Titus ought to flex the muscle of his authority as a leader in a way that shows he's the boss and folks had better understand that he's the boss, but rather a few verses prior, Paul explains how Titus' authority would be established, displayed, and subsequently acknowledged and accepted:

> Show yourself in all respects to be a model of good works, and in your teaching show integrity, dignity, and sound speech that cannot be condemned, so that an opponent may be put to shame, having nothing evil to say about us. (2:7-8)

Titus' authority is substantiated not just by his official title, but by a life that displays the worthy character that seeks after and is set upon Godly truth. This instruction from Paul is not just for Titus. Paul gives the same encouragement to young Pastor Timothy in 1 Timothy 4:12:

> Command and teach these things. Let no one despise you for your youth, but set the believers an example in speech, in conduct, in love, in faith, in purity.

So, in other words, Godly character commands respect, and the chances are good in any particular congregation that a steward of such Godliness who holds respect will also end up serving as a leader with certain measures of authority.

Perhaps you know such people in your congregation. They're the ones who are mindful of the ultimate source of their authority—Jesus Christ—and with that, they are not self-seeking, but rather are serving God's people in faithfulness as they serve the Lord in faithfulness. And the substance of that authority is fed and owned by Godly character—character itself being fed and owned by the capacity to abide by Godly convictions built on the truth of Christ and His Word even when faced with the temptation to forsake God's Word because their reason appears more sensible.

I'm sure you have these people in your church. I'm sure because God provides such goodness for His people. Just like the streams of the springtime sun, He casts the bright beams of His love upon all in His care through the diligent work of faithful servants.

✝

Taking Aim Past Epiphany

For I decided to know nothing among you except Jesus Christ and him crucified. —1 Corinthians 2:2

"I don't like Lent," one person said. "There's too much doom and gloom."

I get it. I do. But here in the final days of Epiphany, as we aim toward Lent, we admit that Lent is in place for such comments. Lent keeps such a perspective from becoming the regular pace of the Christian life. Lent makes sure that we know the measure of the cost, and the significance of our inabilities in the face of that cost so that we don't lose sight of the wonder of the cross and the empty tomb. Those who know me well have heard me say before that if you do not know the seriousness of the bad news—if your church and her preachers and teachers shy from the topics of sin and death and the stranglehold of Satan for the loftier clouds of spiritual sentimentality—you will be robbed of the joy and depth of the Good News.

Lent feels heavier than Epiphany. It feels heftier than Christmas and the Trinity season. Just know that while many may dodge the grittier nature of the message the rest of the year, it's nearly impossible to do so during Lent. Each Sunday in Lent, you can count on hearing from the heavy hitters of Scripture—the texts that clobber us—sometimes leaving us feeling as though we may be getting a lot more Law than Gospel. They'll take stamina to get through, that is if you're willing to listen in the first place.

But not to worry. The Gospel will most certainly be there. Still, it'll be a Gospel that is in no way absent the substance of its value. Take for example the text of Isaiah 53:4, which you're sure to hear:

> Surely he hath borne our griefs and carried our sorrows.

Luther offers so succinctly in connection to these words:

> These are clear and powerful words. The sufferings of this king are our griefs and sorrows. He carries the burden which ought to be ours forever. The stripes and bruises which we have merited, namely, that we should suffer thirst and hunger, and die eternally, all this is laid on Him. His suffering avails for me and for you and for us all; for it was undertaken for our good. (W.A. 34. I. 264 f.)

Luther has a way of cutting through any fog we might have when it comes to God's Word. He's right. The words are powerful. In a very short sentence, we are told that as Jesus suffered and eventually ended up on the cross, all our burdens were His to carry—both the natural consequences of a world coming undone in sin, but also the very real punishment we deserve because of our active disobedience. Jesus didn't shrink from these things, but He embraced them, taking them onto Himself and paying the price in our place.

This all sounds like old-hat Gospel, but each time I hear it, most especially before venturing out into a world wracked by these realities, it changes me. It changes my perspective on the people I run into, the people that I serve, and the people that, in some ways, serve me. It helps me to realize that every individual was on the Divine mind while He hung on the cross. It's impossible to fully comprehend, but He was thinking of you. He was thinking of me. He was thinking of the people around us.

God willing, Lent is helping to calibrate our thoughts in such a way—that is, to know the actual cost for sin and death, so that we might be made ready to rejoice—to be truly joyful in the Easter victory.

Yes, you will hear the bad news of your sin, but I'm willing to wager that your pastor won't keep the Good News from you. If you hear of Jesus' death and resurrection for your rescue, you've heard the powerful Gospel, and that message has the power to convert and convince the heart and bring a joy unequal to anything else this life has to offer.

Listen for it. I'm certain it will be there.

LENT

Don't Avoid Ash Wednesday

If we confess our sins, he is faithful and just to forgive us our sins and to cleanse us from all unrighteousness. —1 John 1:9

L ent begins with Ash Wednesday—the day in the Church Year when the nave and sanctuary are draped in black, and we are, perhaps more so than any other day, drawn to penitent recognition that within the divine courtroom, God has a case against all of us in our sin.

There are plenty of things people choose to avoid seeing and hearing. They do so for various reasons. We all know the reason people avoid the discussion on sin. It hurts. It's the one thing in this life that none of us can escape—not through ducking and covering, not through quick-witted and convincing talk, not by all-out avoidance. Sin finds us, and it does so easily. Why? Because it's already in us. "If we say we have no sin, we deceive ourselves and the truth is not in us" (1 John 1:8). We take the sin-nature with us wherever we go, and like a spiritual slime, we prove ourselves capable of leaving a trail of it behind.

Some might say that to try to avoid this reality is the depth of sin's reflection, but I'd say that to knowingly avoid it is the deeper point in sin's dark trench. If you know you need rescue but are equally unwilling to admit it and seek after help, you are an accomplice to your unfortunate demise.

God would not have it this way. "If we confess our sins, He is faithful and just to forgive us our sins and to cleanse us from all unrighteousness" (1 John 1:9). This is the deeper, lovelier dimension to what is one of the most somber events in the Church Year. On

Ash Wednesday, the job of the preacher is to make sure that you know—unequivocally, unmistakably, unreservedly—that you are a sinner, and the wage for sin is nothing less than eternal death. You will be staged for this truth by an ashen mark in the shape of a cross on your forehead while hearing the words, "Remember that you are dust and to dust you shall return" (Genesis 3:19). But then you will hear how in the deepest reaches of your forsakenness, by a cross, Jesus Christ reached down and took your place in the divine courtroom. He stepped forth from eternity and took the judgment into Himself in every single way, with all of its brute force, and He rescued you.

He would not have you lost but rather found. He would not leave you dead, but alive. He would not see you punished for your crimes but rather freed to be His child of grace in this world.

I encourage you to go to the Lord's house on Ash Wednesday. If you have other plans, cancel them. This is more important. Participate in the ancient ceremony of the Imposition of Ashes. Gather with your church family to recall the common and worldwide dreadfulness of our fall into sin, but do so prepared to receive the Good News of deliverance through the life, death, and resurrection of Jesus Christ for the sins of that same world. Be there to consume that same Good News by way of the Lord's body and blood in the Lord's Supper, a meal that delivers the forgiveness of sins as it reaches in all directions and ages, flowing unbound to you from the divine Son of God who hung on that cross.

Don't avoid Ash Wednesday. If you don't have a church home and you're feeling the tug to find one, give me a call at Our Savior in Hartland, Michigan. I'll do what I can to help you find Christians to kneel beside. I'll do what I can to put you into a church family so that you, like them, will be drawn forward in God's house to be marked with a gritty cross. You're certain to hear the Gospel preached in a place like that. You'll know the depth of the Lord's efforts of love. You'll be able to embrace it.

I guarantee it will change you on the inside, and it will be well worth your while.

✠

Make Your Stand

The night is far gone; the day is at hand. So then let us cast off the works of darkness and put on the armor of light. —Romans 13:12

One morning in the Sunday morning adult Bible study, there was something very Lenten-esque that my group happened upon during the discussion. We talked a little bit about the Greek word ὅπλα, which is translated in both the ESV and the NIV as "armor" and yet is also reliably translated as "weapons." The verse in particular where we met this term was Romans 13:12 where Paul boldly encourages us to be rid of the works of darkness and to put on the ὅπλα of light.

From this, there were a few very important points made during this discussion.

The first is that when Paul speaks of "putting on," he is using the same word he used in Galatians 3:27 where he said that all who have been baptized into Christ, have *been clothed in* or *put on* Christ. That is important for us to know. It is a hint as to the source of the ὅπλα of light. In our baptism, we are clothed in the victory of the One who is the Light of the world, Jesus Christ, and His life, death, and resurrection. Baptized into Him, we are divinely armed.

In Ephesians 6:10-18, Paul defines the armament, calling it the πανοπλίαν (the full weaponry) of God.

Another point of the discussion was for us to keep within the framework and consistency of Paul's words. What I mean is that whether we use the word "weapons" or "armor," both are defensive and offensive by nature. Visiting again with Ephesians 6, verse 11 in particular, Paul describes the motion of those who are dressed in these wartime accessories. Very specifically does he say that to be clad in the armor/weapons of God, is to be made ready for engagement—that is, "so that you can take your stand against the devil's schemes." But again, there's an interesting word being used here. The phrase "take your stand" (στῆναι πρὸς—stand toward) isn't a shaky description of stance. It is an expression of confident strength. It infers forward momentum—the digging in of one's posture and pressing into what's coming. In other words, it isn't reactionary. It means to face off with the foe, to lean into his attacks. Again, in a military sense, it carries a substance of being both defensive and offensive.

So, what's the point?

It all comes back to baptism. Your baptism is a powerfully re-creative thing. Not only have you been joined to Christ—having been made a member of that great body who stands before the throne of God's grace, having a washed robe made bright white in the blood of the Lamb (Revelation 7)—but you have been fortified as one ready to engage in the world with a posture of unearthly courage and strength that proves unbending against the evil schemes of that old evil foe, the devil, who would see the Gospel light dimmed and your hope extinguished.

Pay attention to the readings during Lent. In one way or another—whether prominent or tiptoeing around the scene in concealment—the devil is present in each one. He had to be. As Jesus made His way to the cross, the devil wanted nothing more than to thwart the Lord's efforts. And not just to stop His saving work, but to keep everyone the Lord met from putting their faith in Him. It's the same for us. The devil is scheming to keep us from the Lord, and he's using every weapon at his disposal to do it.

But we have weapons, too. Paul pointed to our baptism as the heavenly weapons cache. Interestingly, when Luther considered some of the same texts, he said that the most deadly of the weapons in that baptismal cache for use by the Christians, the ones capable of slaying the devil, are the Word of God and the regular study of it. Who can argue with that? In essence, Luther just said that the frontline for the supernatural warfare is played out in holy worship, the event where we are immersed from head to toe in the verbal and visible Word of God; and then Bible study, the place where we dig into and embrace that Word for the benefit of salvation and for leaning into the earth-shaking might of the oncoming forces of this present age every single day of our lives.

A lot of folks practice fasting for Lent, that is, they give up something. How about giving up whatever your typical after-worship routine might be and attending the adult Bible study with so many others in your Christian brigade, instead?

It will be worth your while. Although, don't feel as though you need to take my word for it. Take the encouragement of Saint Paul and Luther.

☩

God's Jurisdiction

Therefore, since we have been justified by faith, we have peace with God through our Lord Jesus Christ. Through him we have also obtained access by faith into this grace in which we stand, and we rejoice in hope of the glory of God. Not only that, but we rejoice in our sufferings, knowing that suffering produces endurance, and endurance produces character, and character produces hope, and hope does not put us to shame, because God's love has been poured into our hearts through the Holy Spirit who has been given to us. —Romans 5:1-5

Maybe you'll agree when I say that in this day and age, we do a pretty good job of writing sin off as no big deal, calling both the badness within us and the badness we produce by different names, hoping to find a way to wiggle out of it. One place where this is particularly evident is in the current popularity of referring to our sin as obsessive behaviors—as results of our genetics or pathology—or as simply disorders or lifestyles different from the mainstream.

I certainly won't argue that the capability for particular sins isn't uniquely written into each of us. It most certainly is. You know your tendencies. I know mine. The problem is the excuse-making that sets itself in place to block the guilt associated with the sins. If we are not to blame, if we are not guilty, then we don't need a Savior and we miss the measure of Christ's expense on the cross. Falling into this devilry, we produce the fruits that accompany such disregard. We find the loopholes we need to never be wrong in any discussion, to never be guilty of an offense in any situation coming undone, to never be the one who isn't carrying his fair share of the load, to never be the one who bears responsibility. In essence, we get to avoid using the word "sin" altogether, as if it applies to everyone else except us.

Sin only makes sense when it is considered within the context of God. In other words, if we are going to understand it rightly, and most especially how it meets with us, then maybe one place to start is with acknowledging the fact that we are under the jurisdiction of an ultimate judge of right and wrong. Whether we like it or not, whether we're willing to admit it or not, we are subject to a divine "Someone" who holds the authority for determining what human conduct is supposed to be.

This may sound somewhat strange, but one of the best aspects of the season of Lent, especially as it is designed to recalibrate us toward objectively true things, is to be confronted with the true nature of sin and what that means for Mankind's future. To know this is to know the need—a very personal need. It is to then be found at the foot of the cross, a place where we can breathe a sigh of relief as having narrowly escaped destruction because the One hanging on that cross paid the price for our deliverance.

Knowing the weight of our sin is a good way to understand the weight of the Gospel of our salvation through Jesus Christ. And that's where we must reside—in the Gospel. The Gospel is powerful. It gives us the ability to confess our sin in true repentance and faith—not to excuse our sin away as a bad habit, or justifiable in certain circumstances, or as nothing at all—but rather to admit whole-heartedly that we are dust and to dust we shall return. It supplies us with a brightly beaming hope in the One who by His work raises us from the dust and sets us into His resurrected life: Jesus Christ, the Son of God!

This is a big part of the theology of Lent. And I pray that this message is resonating with you, that you are embracing it and carrying it forth into the world around you. With this supernatural knowledge pacing through your spirit, you'd be amazed at how the sun shines a little more brightly and the days are just a little more splendid, even when facing some pretty hefty struggles in this world.

✠

Mom and Dad: Keep At It!

Go therefore and make disciples of all nations, baptizing them in the name of the Father and of the Son and of the Holy Spirit, teaching them to observe all that I have commanded you. And behold, I am with you always, to the end of the age. —Matthew 28:19-20

I love being able to look around the church nave and see children of all ages. Indeed, it serves the heart well. This is true because it means moms and dads are taking very seriously the Lord's words in Matthew 28:19-20 where He instructs and emphasizes that Christians are made through the two-fold event of washing with water and the Word (Baptism) combined with a regular diet of all that the Lord has given (teaching). Baptizing and teaching are inseparable parts of the same mandate.

To put this into perspective, if someone were to come to me and ask that I baptize his or her child, and yet would state an unwillingness to raise the child in the Christian faith, I would say no. I'd have to. Baptizing and teaching go together. You can't have one without the other.

So, when I look around the church during worship and I see the little ones with their parents, it always makes me smile. It reminds me of the living faith that Christ gave those parents in their baptism, and it points all of us to a horizon where we see the next generation equipped to do the same.

It also makes me want to help those families with children in any way that I can. It's one reason why in my church we stock the pews with the booklet resource entitled *Kids in the Divine Service (https://www.lcms.org/worship/kids-in-the-divine-service)*. These are designed to be a helpful resource for teaching the why-we-do-what-we-do of the life of faith in worship. It's also why we encourage parents to take the kids out when they get a little rowdy but then to bring them back in as soon as they are ready. Sure, every kid gets restless, and so when they decide to bang the hymnal against the pew, or shout at the top of their lungs, or run their Tonka truck up and down the hardwood pew, that can be incredibly loud and distracting, and so it's a good idea to take them out in respect for others. But once the appropriate recalibration has happened, get them right back into the church as soon as possible. The little ones belong in there with the rest of their Christian family—with their Savior, Jesus Christ.

Are there other things a congregation can do as a community to help parents? You bet! The community can be sure to hug mom and say, "Keep at it," or pat dad on the back and say, "Good job." These gestures and words make a difference. I know they helped me and my wife, Jennifer, when our kids were smaller.

Another thing to keep in mind (and it's something that many folks with older children already know so well) is that so often parents of little ones feel as though they are working so hard and doing all they can just to get to and keep the child in worship, all the while feeling as though as parents, they aren't getting anything out of the service because they're so busy with the child. This is a very real concern, and it's one that when I hear it, I not only do what I can to encourage the parents—reminding them that this is a very important time in their life when faithfulness to Christ in holy worship looks and feels less like something spiritual and more like riot control. Still, they are being faithful to Christ in their service, and He by no means intends to leave the parents out of the blessings being bestowed to the whole Christian family in the worship setting. With this, I also try to remind them that the Word of God is so much more powerful than we often give credit. When it comes to worship, being there immersed in the liturgy, which is entirely comprised of God's Word, is by no means an empty experience for the Christian. To this, in a practical sense, I try to add that for most who come to worship regularly, the liturgy gets written into the heart and mind in a way that allows a mom or dad to do mom or dad things and still receive. Because of the liturgy, the service becomes more or less memorized, and now mom and dad can follow along and be fed without needing to juggle a hymnal, ordo, baby bottle, and infant all at the same time. They become people who live and breathe the words of worship, and what better example do we want to display for our kids than this?

Thanks be to God for the little ones in your worshipping community! Thanks be to God for the parents who stick with it, who give it their all to make sure that their baptized children are being raised in the Christian faith. "Therefore, my beloved brothers," Paul said, "be steadfast, immovable, always abounding in the work of the Lord, knowing that in the Lord your labor is not in vain" (1 Corinthians 15:58). Of all efforts in the Church, perhaps the job of parents doing all they can to get their kids to and keep them in worship is most appreciated by this text. To such folks I say: Know that I'm rooting for you, and so are many others in our midst.

✠

Now He Took Courage

Now he took courage and went to Pilate and asked for the body of Jesus.
—Mark 15:43

E very year in my congregation during the season of Lent, we read through the Passion Narrative drawn from the four Gospels. For me, it is always an exceptionally moving event. As the one called to stand before God's people and read it, I sometimes struggle. Every year I choke a little at certain moments, doing my best to keep the sadness from seeping over and into my voice and facial expressions. I mean, what use is a weeping clergyman in the middle of a service? Although, I'm sure it's a sight well worth experiencing for some. It certainly has the potential for displaying your pastor's sense of God's Word.

There is a portion of the narrative that begins with Jesus being assigned to His cross, and it ends with Pilate shooing away the Pharisees who continue to pester him even after the body of Jesus is in the tomb and the stone has been sealed, this time asking for guards to be stationed at the sepulcher lest the disciples come and steal away the body and tell everyone that Jesus arose. In between these monumental moments, there were two instances in particular that catch my attention.

The first comes by way of the phrase, "Those who had known Him stood at a distance, as also the women who had followed Him" (Luke 23:49).

Even as I'm reading these words publically I'll be sorting through to the thought that we are to know by these words that Jesus went into the battle of all battles completely and utterly alone. The disciples had scattered, and if any had turned back to brave the scene, they did so from a place of personal safety, a place where they could see the Son of God on the cross without seeing the blood-soaked details, without seeing the immensity of the sacrifice as He gave Himself over in totality for the sins of the world. Even the women who had gathered near to the cross, and the disciple John, whom Jesus, in shortness of breath, gave as a son to His mother Mary, even they had moved away into the distance, unable to bear the event.

The dreadful enormity of Jesus' cry "My God, My God, why have you forsaken me?" (Matthew 27:46) comes into incredible focus. The pull of the scene's gravity is felt.

The second phrase that often catches my eye arrives a few paragraphs later. Joseph of Arimathea is unfavorably noted as not having consented to the purpose of the Sanhedrin and yet was one who kept his faith in Jesus a secret for fear of what his fellow Jews might do to him if they discovered it. We are to know by this that Joseph did nothing to defend the innocence of Jesus. We are to know that when the mocking and spitting and pummeling began, Joseph was there, but he turned away, too.

And then suddenly, just as the hope in this description of Joseph is snuffed, the tenor changes and we learn something happened to him when he saw the Savior sentenced and ultimately killed. We read, "Now he took courage and went to Pilate and asked for the body of Jesus" (Mark 15:43).

Now he took courage.

Again, while reading this text publically to God's people, I managed to sort through to the realization that even as the cross is a stumbling stone of offense, it is also the moment of moments situated at the heart of a message with the power to turn the world backward on its axis. Even before the resurrection could be added to its glory, it penetrated Joseph's fear and it gave to him valor for streaming past what would have been the Sanhedrin's desire for irreverent disposal of the criminal Jesus' remains and to go straight to the civil authorities, to Pilate, to request the body for burial.

The Sanhedrin would know what he did. The ruling civil authority already in disposition against Jesus and His followers would have his name and know who he was. His life of safety and respect and honor and comfort in the community was about to come undone.

Now he took courage.

Most merciful God, grant that I would not keep my distance from the Lord and His cross, but that it would be well known that I am a believer who fears not the principalities of this world but only unfaithfulness to the One who so faithfully won my eternity. In the holy and most precious name of Jesus I plead. Amen.

✝

The Salt of the Earth

You are the salt of the earth, but if salt has lost its taste, how shall its saltiness be restored? It is no longer good for anything except to be thrown out and trampled under people's feet. You are the light of the world. A city set on a hill cannot be hidden. Nor do people light a lamp and put it under a basket, but on a stand, and it gives light to all in the house. In the same way, let your light shine before others, so that they may see your good works and give glory to your Father who is in heaven. —Matthew 5:13-16

Considering the Lord's words in Matthew 5:13-16, it becomes difficult to deny that we are often the means by which God blesses the world around us with that which will ultimately point others to the only One who can save them: Jesus Christ.

Why does this matter?

Because not only do the Lord's words in the text include you—that is if you are a believer—but they encourage you to take seriously what Lent has been teaching you. "Get in the game," they urge. Engage with those around you. Do this knowing that you are blessed as a servant of the One who fully intends to use your efforts for faithfulness, both in word and deed, to extend His kingdom to others who need saving.

And He'll do all of this to His glory.

This truth in particular feeds me with hope for each new day, and it reminds me to remind you of the same so that you would share in that peace.

✠

To Know Nothing Else

But we preach Christ crucified. —1 Corinthians 1:23

P alm Sunday begins the journey through the city streets of Jerusalem into the events of Holy Week. When it comes to an end, we'll find ourselves situated at the foot of Good Friday's cross.

That's where we're going.

In a sense, as Christians, that's always where we're going—to the foot of Good Friday's cross. Every day, by way of our baptism into Christ, we are those who stand alongside the preaching of Saint Paul when he declares, "For I decided to know nothing among you except Jesus Christ and him crucified" (1 Corinthians 2:2).

Why does he say it this way?

Because there on the cross, we not only see the results of Mankind's innermost nature in sin—the immense cost of all that we are as fallen creatures—but we also see in that grotesque sight the most beautiful of occurrences: the Hope of the nations, the Rescuer of the lost, the Redeemer of the entire cosmos willingly submitting Himself to being spiked to wood as the perfect sacrifice.

This image will never be fully mined of its significance in this life. Countless theologians throughout the ages have tried to get to the absolute bottom of Calvary's depths, but in the end, have all been forced to settle with the vocabulary and limitations of human language. Still, the power of the image, as it feeds faith, has provided for the right words to be put into the right order to create opportunities for the Church to sing hymns like "Jesus, Priceless Treasure." By such sacred hymnody, the Church calls out words like, "Yet, though sin and hell assail me, Jesus will not fail me," followed by, "Satan, I defy thee; Death I now decry thee; Fear I bid thee cease!"

Only by way of Christ's outpouring on the cross can we sing these things with the confidence they intend.

As with other theologians in history, Luther tried to simplify the image when he wrote things like:

> "Look at this picture and love it. There is no greater bondage or form of service than that the Son of God should be the servant and should bear the sin of every man, however poor and wretched or despised. What an amazing thing it would be if some king's son should go into a beggar's hut to nurse him in his illness, wash off his filth and do all the things which otherwise the beggar would have to do. All the world would gape with open mouths, noses, ears, and eyes, and could never think and talk enough about it. Would that not be a wonderful humility?... But behold, what does it mean? The Son of God becomes my servant and humbles Himself, saying to me: 'You are no longer a sinner, but I, I Myself step into your place. You have not sinned; I have. The whole world lies in sin, but you are not in sin, but I am. All your sin shall be upon Me, and not on you.' No man can comprehend it. In this life hereafter we shall have a knowledge of the love of God and gaze upon it in eternal blessedness." (Exposition of John I, W.A. 46. 680 f.)

Of course, Luther is right, and as I said, we'll never fully understand the vast dimensions of what was happening that day on that dreadful hill outside of Jerusalem's walls, a Friday we now call "good." Still, Lent has been helping us. It is in place to keep before us the Word of God, which reveals to us our frailty and offers the supercharged Gospel of salvation through the One who took our place in judgment.

Yes, the message is vast and powerful, but as Luther explained, it can be held so close in relative simplicity. Jesus died for you. By this act, He took your sins on Himself. Through faith in Him and His sacrifice, all is well and you have eternal life.

Thanks be to God for this! Thanks be to God for the freedom to live in this each day by the power of the Holy Spirit!

Good Friday

Put Away Your Fraudulence

Look at the birds of the air: they neither sow nor reap nor gather into barns, and yet your heavenly Father feeds them. Are you not of more value than they? —Matthew 6:26

My wife, Jennifer, is becoming more and more skilled at capturing images of the various birds that make their way to the feeder near one of our living room windows. As her husband—a pastor with a mind for the visuals of language— her images are sermonic in a sense. First, they speak the Law, which is to say that as the whole world has become undone by sin, a simple reminder of this is that even a bird has to eat. Every hungry stomach rumbles. None are wholly self-sufficient. All living things need help from the outside or else they'll perish.

But the images of the birds also speak a Christ-centered Gospel, just as Christ said they would. They are distilled moments to ponder what our Lord has so kindly urged. Look at these tiny creatures adorned with colored crowns and feathered wings. Recall that they neither sow nor reap nor gather into barns, and yet the heavenly Father feeds them. Behold a God who cares even for the simplest of his creatures. Are you not of more value than they?

Oh, yes, you are!

The proof of your value is there on the cross in all of its gory detail. God has reached into this world through the person and work of Jesus Christ. And His Word is that this death was not for the birds, but rather for you.

Set aside your fraudulent self-sufficiency. Own the need of which a rumbling stomach warns. You need complete rescue from the outside. The cross displays that rescue. Go see for yourself. See the Savior die that you would live forever. This the epicenter of the approaching Good Friday message for you, as even a bird at the feeder serves to remind.

☩

EASTER

The Counterpunch

He is not here, for he has risen, as he said. Come, see the place where he lay. —Matthew 28:6

S everal years ago a particularly beloved matriarch of my congregation was killed in an automobile accident. Her name was Lorraine. For most in the parish, Lorraine's death left an unfillable hole in their hearts. She was incredibly vibrant and ever-so-lovely in her life of faith—not only serving her Lord and His people with such joy but doing so with what seemed like unearthly stamina. She was always ready and on-call to meet the needs of others, no matter what they might be, and she did so with a smile that could peel back even the thickest covering on the hardest of hearts.

I know many still miss her. I know I still do. With that, I want to share something about her that I, as her pastor, knew and rather appreciated.

Lent and Easter were her favorite times of the Church Year.

Of course, like most faithful Christians, Christmas was a favorite time for Lorraine. But even so, she made sure that I knew she adored the seasons of Lent and Easter. And why? Because of what sits at the heart of these pinnacle seasons: The precise spectrum of the death of the sinless Son of God for her sins and the sins of the whole world, and the cracking open of a tomb at Easter that was powerless to hold in everlasting darkness that same Lord. Lorraine loved the very potent imagery of Ash Wednesday—the palling of ash upon man as a reminder of the need for rescue—and the 40 days that follow leading to Easter, having at their core the somber reality of what our loving Lord would do so that we would not be lost to sin, but rather would be delivered through His person and work.

Lent and Easter were sobering seasons for Lorraine, and she appreciated that her church didn't handle them carelessly. She was glad to be carried into them on the tails of deep meaning, knowing that every rite and ceremony was in place to help keep the eyes of God's people on the Lord's work. When Good Friday was at its deepest and darkest, Lorraine was ready for the Baptismal flame of the Easter Vigil to be kindled the very next day, knowing that she was being ushered into a new time, a new day—Easter!—a day that certifies all that Jesus did to save us as certain and true!

In the resurrection of Jesus, everything is different now. Death is disarmed. We are no longer its hostages. No wonder Lorraine would so dearly love this apex of the cosmic drama. It's the very work of Jesus on display for our eternal life!

Ash Wednesday gave us the hardest, most gripping news. Lent carried this into its depths. Good Friday showed us the price tag. Easter is the counter-punch to all of it. It heralds the victory, the most joyous action of God on your behalf. It is truly the celebration of all celebrations.

No wonder Lorraine loved it so much. And thanks be to God that the Lord's Easter victory is hers right now in its absolute fullness.

☩

Obedience to the King

Blessed is the man who remains steadfast under trial, for when he has stood the test he will receive the crown of life, which God has promised to those who love him. —James 1:12

There's a book I use both devotionally and as a supplement to the life of prayer in my congregation. Its title is *Minister's Prayer Book*. It is a gathering of meditative gems compiled by John W. Doberstein. I read something in the volume that I wanted to share with you. It was just one sentence from a man by the name of Abraham Kuyper.

Kuyper was a late nineteenth and early twentieth-century journalist and Calvinist theologian. Now, while I don't subscribe to Calvinist theology, just as my Lutheran tradition takes and uses the good portions from across history, I took a small piece of something good from Kuyper's words. He wrote:

> An office-bearer who wants something other than to obey his King is unfit to bear his office.

Kuyper was speaking of pastors in particular. And he was right. If pastors venture into the Office of the Holy Ministry seeking anything other than to be faithful to Christ no matter the challenges, they are disqualified. But then as I read this, reality set in. God calls sinful human beings—men—into this office. Human beings are sinful. I speak from experience. In my sinful flesh, like you, I am more than capable of finding myself seeking something other than obedience to Jesus.

So what to do? Am I disqualified? No.

At the heart of the sentence, and in its fuller context, is the intent to warn pastors to wrestle with the flesh, being certain that Christ's way dominates in the pastor's efforts. How does this happen? By clinging to His Word. When I feel as though I should do things my way, or preach what I want, or act in the Church in a way that seizes authority from my Lord and strays from His Word, I must be certain to remember to be led by the truest authority—the One I serve who gives and guides by and through His Word.

In a sense, it's the same for you. The Word of God shapes you, not the other way around. When you don't like what it says, contemplate the premise that its ways and wisdom will always far surpass the ways of Man. That means you. That means me. We don't like to hear this because, sometimes, it hurts. But for the Christian, I would surmise that more often it has the potential for stirring joy. Either way, remember that it is good and it is best. Why? Well, that's a rhetorical question. We both know the answer.

✝

Hope's Feathers

And we boast in the hope of the glory of God. —Romans 5:2

Emily Dickinson is by far one of my favorite poets. She had an incredible grasp of language; and not only that, but she could string together a necklace of words with such uncommon precision, and pair nearly every phrase with incredible rhyme schemes. It's hard not to appreciate her skill. I have a volume that includes her entire collection of works, and I must say, I visit with it often. And even as I read her poetry knowing that she wasn't necessarily a Christian—although she grew up in a Christian home and was influenced by Christian tradition—her words ring true in many ways, whether she realized it or not. For example, a personal favorite of her lyrics goes something like this:

> "Hope" is the thing with feathers—
> That perches in the soul—
> And sings the tune without the words—
> And never stops—at all—

I like that. Hope perches in the soul and never stops singing its song. Sounds like the hope we have in Jesus if you ask me. By the power of the Holy Spirit through the Gospel, hope lives and breathes and moves within us even as we face days of both sunshine and rain, of blue skies and clouds. Or as Saint Paul says in Romans 5:1-5:

> Therefore, since we have been justified through faith, we have peace with God through our Lord Jesus Christ, through whom we have gained access by faith into this grace in which we now stand. And we boast in the hope of the glory of God. Not only so, but we also glory in our sufferings, because we know that suffering produces

97

perseverance; perseverance, character; and character, hope. And hope does not put us to shame, because God's love has been poured out into our hearts through the Holy Spirit, who has been given to us.

One more time: "And we boast in the hope of the glory of God" (v. 2). I like that, too.

Paul's words speak of hope as it flows from God's glory. You and I know by the Holy Word that the truest form of God's glory is seen on the cross in the death of Jesus Christ for our forgiveness—at least that's the way Jesus talked about it (John 12:23-33; Mark 10:36-38, and others).

And I'm also fond of this: "And hope does not put us to shame, because God's love has been poured out into our hearts through the Holy Spirit, who has been given to us." Here Paul makes sure we understand that our hope in the suffering, crucified, and risen Savior is never to our shame, but rather it is the wellspring of God's love that pours into our hearts to steady our resolve and sturdy our grasp of the only One who can save us—Christ, the Son of God!

May this hope continue to be yours as the spring days unfold in preparation for summer. Remember to hold fast to the means by which God feeds and sustains this hope—Word and Sacrament ministry. You need these things. I need these things. The whole world needs these things. Why? Because it has what sets hope in the soul where it can sing and sing and sing, never growing tired of its joyful song of salvation.

✠

The Deepest of All Sorrows

Truly, truly, I say to you, you will weep and lament, but the world will rejoice. You will be sorrowful, but your sorrow will turn into joy. —John 16:20

I read a portion from Luther yesterday that still rings today. Concerning John 16:20, he writes:

> There are many kinds of sorrow on earth, but the deepest of all sorrows is when the heart loses Christ, and He is no longer seen, and there is no hope or comfort from Him. (W.A. 49. 258. ff.)

I expect that most Christians would nod in agreement. And why is this? Because by faith, they know things that the rest of the world doesn't.

They know that without Christ, there is no hope. They know that apart from Him, there is the extreme incapability for joy among this world's terrors. They know that to be apart from Him is to be starved of the nourishing forgiveness and grace that He would have for His own. He desires to give this sustaining love so that we would be His own and live under Him in joy.

When the heart loses this, there is emptiness.

Very soon the warmer days of summer will arrive. With those days will come the plentiful opportunities to take a break from being where Christ is given through Word and Sacrament for the strengthening of faith and the fruits of comforting hope.

Resist the temptation to stay away from worship. It can only harm you. On the other hand, be encouraged to remain faithful in worship throughout the summer months. Embrace every opportunity to be where Christ is with His gifts—most especially when you go away on vacation. Even when you're out of town, don't hide the Lord from yourself or your family, but instead, take a moment and talk to your pastor. Let him know where you'll be. The odds are good that he'll know of a welcoming congregation being served by a faithful pastor who will be glad to serve you with the heavenly gifts that can cure the deepest of sorrows and make sturdier the hope you have in Jesus.

✠

The Experts and Jesus

And when Jesus had finished speaking, he said to Simon, "Put out into the deep and let down your nets for a catch." —Luke 5:4

C ommon sense often has very little to do with the Christian faith. Here's what I mean.

Considering the Lord's words to Simon Peter in Luke 5:4, the fishing night, the time when fishing would be accomplished, had passed. Jesus had traveled to Lake Gennesaret (which is also the Sea of Galilee). He's been followed by crowds of people pressing in around Him, and as the text says so succinctly, they are doing this because they want to hear the Word. It's there by the shore that Jesus meets Peter, along with James and John. They're fishermen, and they're calling it quits just as He approaches—washing their nets and packing up their boats and tools with nothing to show from a long night of work.

Jesus climbs into Peter's boat and asks him to push out into the shallows.

Strange.

I remember chatting about this with my friend, Pastor Jakob Heckert, not long before he died. I remember the two of us thinking it seemed rude on the Lord's part to make this request of Peter, especially since Peter had just come in from a long night of fishing. He was likely exhausted, and if he was anything like the rest of us (and we know he was), he just wanted to go home and rest.

But so strangely, Peter doesn't resist Jesus' request. Perhaps out of respect for the Rabbi, he does what he asks. No big deal. What's another hour, right?

With that, Jesus preaches to the people, and as He concludes, He turns to Peter and his assistants and stretches the boundaries of their hospitality a little further. Jesus tells Peter to let down the nets into the deep water for a catch. It's at this point in the story that I can almost hear Peter give out a sigh as he thinks, "Wait a minute. I'm tired. We're tired. We worked all night and caught nothing. The best time for fishing has long since passed, and with that, we're done. And you saw us packing up and cleaning our nets, right? Do you honestly expect us to go through the trouble of dragging them out and casting them again, especially during the most inopportune time to fish? Don't you realize what a colossal failure that would be?"

A colossal failure. Sounds and feels very familiar to me. Why? Because I've had my share. And I often find myself convinced that with a little bit of common sense, I can avoid future failures by doing this or that. In one sense that's true. But in another, it couldn't be any further from the truth.

This carries us to what we know of the power of the Gospel. As believers—people converted and convinced by the Gospel—we are those who live and die trusting in the powerful Word of Jesus of Nazareth, who, when He speaks, does not give empty words even as we recognize that His Word won't always jive with what we are thinking needs to be done in any particular situation. Believers are living proof of this wonderful trust. So often we continue in holy worship—Sunday after Sunday—no matter what the secular world may try to tell us, no matter how tired we are from the previous day's efforts, no matter what common sense might urge as better use of our time and resources. Instead, we continue to gather because the Gospel Word of Jesus has power and it has changed us. It is for us the greatest story ever told, and it is a message of hope and deliverance we can trust even when it sends us out onto the deep water to drop our nets. We do this even as common sense, experience, and all the experts say there won't be any fish.

The Gospel had this very same effect on Peter. He'd been carried to a point where it would have made sense for him as the fishing expert to seize control of the situation and advise the Lord in a better way. But he'd heard the preached Word of the Gospel before Jesus called for the impossible. Peter, a man who had been cultivated by Jesus' preaching, could not end his sentence to Jesus about the long day and the cleaning of the nets with a response of refusal. Instead, he says so simply, "We have fished all night and caught nothing, but at Your Word, I will let down the nets."

And then we watch Peter very closely. We watch what the world would call foolishness. Peter will trust the Lord, and he will witness the catch of fish and then he will fall to his knees in confession, asking the Lord to leave his presence because Simon is a sinful man and unworthy of being near Him. And still, thanks be to Jesus, He doesn't agree with Peter's common-sense advice. Instead, He stays with him and absolves him, "Do not be afraid, Simon. From now on, you will be a catcher of men!" In other words, you are forgiven, and now by the power of the Holy Spirit in this same Gospel, you will preach a Word that matches the backward events of this day. You will preach the powerful Gospel of Christ crucified!

It wasn't that many years ago that an expert warned me, as they warned other churches and schools, if we didn't change course and become more palatable to the world, we would almost certainly close our doors. But here we are many years after the prediction. Sure, we have our struggles, but one thing is for sure: *The so-called experts have nothing on Jesus.*

Even better, when I think about these things, I'm glad for the Lord's words in Luke 5. I need to hear and remember them. These words are a Gospel-filled encouragement to continue in faithful stewardship with the gifts the Lord provides, trusting Him and seeking only faithfulness to Him, even as the world around us continues to tell us that we need to do this and that, to use the Law to frighten and bring guilt and shame to motivate givers and attenders. The Lord doesn't say those kinds of things. Instead, by His Word, He preaches, "Keep Word and Sacrament in this place, and be sure to keep them pure. That's what makes Christians. From that, be strengthened, be patient, and teach my people to be Christians. Lift them by the Gospel of forgiveness that they may know not only the joy of giving back to the One who gave everything for them, but they may know My love, that they would share this love, that they would seek first the Kingdom in all things, and they would be with Me in the eternal joys of paradise."

So, with that, I say "Thanks be to God there are Christians who, when their trust is called "foolish," their first inclination is to smile and say innocently, "You should read Luke 5 because so is fishing in broad daylight in the deep water."

At Your Word, dear Jesus, I will continue to trust you even when it doesn't make sense. And by the power of the Holy Spirit through Your Gospel, I will let down my net for a catch.

✠

He First Loved Us

We love because he first loved us. —1 John 4:19

My youngest daughter, Evelyn, mentioned that her favorite week of the summer break is the first one after the last day of school. I just have to say that I think I agree, although, even though I'm glad for the slower schedule, I do miss the high-fives, hugs, and loving interaction with the students in my congregation's day school. It's always a strange and alien thing to see the hallways of the school empty and then also to experience the silence of that emptiness.

Still, I'm not going to trade away the coming summer. I love the summertime. Heck, feel free to add a month or two to it.

John speaks to both divine and human love in 1 John 4:19. Thinking more deeply about this, I realize just how jam-packed John's sentence truly is.

For some, it might sound (at first) as though it is describing solely what we do. You need to know that it isn't. Its drive is the love of God for us. Read the sentence out loud and listen. He first loved us. Now we love.

That's the Gospel.

I'm sure if I sat down right now to start tapping away at the words of a sermon on this text, by God's grace, the Holy Spirit would show how these words are aimed squarely at the cross of Jesus Christ. From the victory won there, I'd tell you all about how we have been recreated to express that love to others.

Still, I would come back to Christ. I'd have to.

We can only love because of His love. Without His love at work in us, the human love we might express becomes empty. The whole point of John's words is our rescue by the One who loved us as no one else ever will or could. That, of course, always leads the believer to the cross knowing that the proclamation of the cross is the fulfillment of God's love through the death of Jesus—all for us, and alive and active through us.

✝

The Seed is Planted

A gentle tongue is a tree of life. —Proverbs 15:4

I'm forever amazed at how God continues to refresh His world through His Christians. There always seems to be plentiful opportunities for Christian communities to move forward together by God's grace, working diligently by the strength He provides for bringing His Gospel message to the world around us—and not just through one particular church's immediate mission efforts, but by the efforts of individuals in their jobs, with their sports teams, in their neighborhoods, and with their families.

Proverbs 15:4 says so eloquently, "A gentle tongue is a tree of life." Another way to translate this is to say "a healing tongue." Healing is God's action, namely, the gift of restoration He gives by His abundant mercy. Christ is the tree of life, and we being the branches, use our human tongues to share His merciful action that saved us from sin, death, and the power of the devil.

In other words, a tongue that brings the restorative message of the Gospel is attached to a splendid and blessed person born of the same message. And the message itself, by the power of the Holy Spirit at work through the Word of the Gospel, gives not only courage but also the best words at the best time and in the best order. It may not necessarily feel like it, but trust that what I tell you is true. God will use you to plant a seed so that, one day, it might grow to His glory and the salvation of the person to whom you are giving it.

✠

Climb the High Dive

For by grace you have been saved through faith. And this is not your own doing; it is the gift of God, not a result of works, so that no one may boast.
—Ephesians 2:8-9

I conducted and then shared with my congregation the results of an informal survey a few weeks after one of our quarterly congregation meetings. I did this for a reason.

Essentially, I called the local Methodist, Baptist, ELCA (Evangelical Lutheran Church in America), two non-denominational churches, and a sister Lutheran Church—Missouri Synod (LCMS) congregation in a nearby township and I asked several questions, one of which was: "What is the process for becoming a member of your congregation?" Here's what I discovered.

The two non-denominational churches I contacted are very similar to one another. Both encourage prospective members to choose and join one of several small groups they call "Life Groups." These groups meet once a week for six weeks and are tailored to be "relevant" to the participants' needs (newly divorced, alcoholics, even sports fans). Again, prospective members are encouraged to join one of these groups, but it is not a requirement for membership. They can join whenever they want.

The Methodist, ELCA, and LCMS churches offer a single, three-hour class. The class takes place as needed on a Saturday. Church leaders are present to meet the prospective members and to talk about the church's structure and membership expectations. Church doctrine is not necessarily discussed, and membership is granted after the session if the participant desires.

The Baptist church does not offer a class. It expects prospective members to learn as they go. A person can join when they decide they are ready.

So, why am I sharing all of this? Because whenever a church starts to talk about money, the topic of attendance and attracting new members never seem to be too far behind. This was true for the quarterly congregation meeting I mentioned at the beginning.

During the discussion surrounding our annual budget proposal, I found myself compelled to urge all in attendance to keep a few things in the proper perspective when it comes to money and membership.

First, I asked folks to consider how the Bible defines healthy stewardship. I offered some basics to show that we are indeed aligned with and practicing these truths. Do we have our struggles? Yes. Are they big? In my opinion, it depends on who you talk to. But big or small, should we worry that we are doing things in an unhealthy way as a congregation? Well, according to the Scriptures, no.

Second, I reminded folks that we cannot necessarily factor "faith" into the financial predictions necessary for preparing a budget. What we can do is identify those things that God allows to stand before us as demanding of our trust in Him—the challenges— or as Luther called them, "tentatio." I pointed out that tentatio is a necessary part of growing as Christians. God uses the tentatio to test and refine His people. They aren't necessarily designed to be pleasant, but God knows best and so He allows His people to be challenged to strengthen hope in Him (Romans 5:1-5). In other words, tentatio isn't necessarily bad!

Next, I asked folks to consider how the Bible says real Christians are made. It is by the power of the Holy Spirit through the Word of the Gospel, both verbal and visible—Word and Sacrament. I urged folks to consider that if they, as individual Christians, are not reaching out to folks around them with the Gospel, we should not expect our pews to fill up too rapidly. I affirmed that, yes, it is true that as the pastor I am called by Christ to this place to preach and teach the Gospel and to administer the Sacraments according to Christ's mandate, but I'm not the only one around here who is called to speak the hope that lives within himself to family, friends, or neighbors while I'm at Walmart, or the car repair shop, or the local restaurant. And while I know for sure others are doing this, still, if there are only a few of us, then, well, I think you get the point.

Finally, I urged that we need to understand that our church is vastly different from the others in the area, which brings me back around to where all of this started. Once our visitors have reached a point where they are willing to invest the time and energy to become a member of our congregation, it takes more than a few hours on a Saturday. A typical new member class takes about ten to fifteen weeks to complete—and the class is by no means shallow. Not only do folks learn the Biblical theology behind the Lord's Supper, Baptism, Christian faith and life, but they learn to discern objective truth by way of the Word of God. For example, they learn the difference between things like *norma normata* and *norma normans*, *exegesis* versus *eisegesis*. It takes a while to do this. But why is it this way? Because as Christians in this place, we take very seriously our Lord's mandate for making Christians. God has made it clear that the people who gather in fellowship together here must know what is taught, believed, and confessed at this altar (1 Corinthians 10:14-22).

Now, having read all of this, take a moment and think about what it is that may be preventing you from consciously reaching out and inviting someone you know to church with you. What is stopping you from helping to fill your church's new member class? Is it fear?

Is it doubt? Maybe you don't think you'll say the right words? Whatever it is, I'll bet the following bits of advice will help.

The initial bit of advice is something I find myself employing quite often in a variety of situations. The one that follows is a Biblical truth for all Christians.

First, climb the ladder to the high dive and jump!

When I was a kid, there was a public pool near my home. It was the rule that once you climbed the ladder to the high dive, the lifeguard would not let you climb back down. The only way down was to jump into the water. One day, I didn't necessarily dare to do it, but somehow I forced myself to climb knowing full well that once I was up there it was out of my control. Think about someone you want to share the Gospel with and then climb the ladder to the high dive. Pick up the phone and dial the number for that person. Let it ring. Since most folks have caller ID, if you chicken out, you will have already passed the point of no return and they will wonder why you called. Or perhaps climbing the high dive means writing a letter. Just do it. Write it, put it into an envelope, put a stamp on it, and then drop it in the mailbox at the post office. You can't get it out now. You're stuck. Or type up an email and hit "send" before your fear causes you to reconsider. You can't get that email back. It's now sitting in the inbox of someone you would love to see beside you in holy worship.

Climb the ladder to the high dive because then you'll have to jump into the water! And if you are like me, after a few jumps, it won't be so scary anymore.

My second bit of advice: Rest assured that it's not your job to convert or convince anyone. It is the job of the Holy Spirit (Ephesians 2:8-9, 1 Corinthians 12:3, Romans 1:16, John 1:12-13, John 3:5-8). There is nothing to fear (Psalm 27:1). Be faithful (Matthew 25:23). Be the Christian God has made you and simply give the message (Matthew 5:13-16, Luke 14:23). God has promised to work through that message to accomplish His purposes (Philippians 2:13). The results are not in your hands. If after you give the message, you find yourself in a discussion that you don't think you can handle, just be honest. Tell the person you don't know the answers to his or her questions. Offer to find out more. Or better yet, let your pastor try! Pass along his phone number or email address. Let him work with you to make the introduction!

If after all of this you feel as though nothing appears to be taking root, don't consider yourself a failure. Remember, Christ Himself was often rejected, even by His own family (John 6:41-71). Instead, keep that person in prayer and be ready. You have given a powerful Gospel. It can change a heart and mind at any moment. Just look at Nicodemus, a devout Pharisee. He received the Gospel (John 3) and was later found defending Jesus before his fellow Pharisees, even to the point of being ridiculed (John 6). And then, of course, Nicodemus can be found at the tomb as a believer preparing the Lord's body for burial near the end of John's Gospel account.

By the way, while you are praying for the Gospel to take root in those with whom you've shared it, set your sights on someone else!

While churches do have seats that are filled, there are always those that are empty. And while I can understand why people gravitate toward thinking that more members just naturally means more offerings, Christians need to keep that sort of thinking as far from their hearts and minds as possible. That is not the right connection to make. The Church isn't after money. Large structures, big budgets, plentiful staffing, many and various programs and activities do not necessarily mean a church is being successful. Christians are called to be faithful. Faithful Christians reach out to the world around them to introduce others to the One who gave His life as the ransom for sin. As they do this, those same Christians trust that God is faithful and will provide all that is necessary for this body and life!

If you are already actively reaching out to others, great! Keep at it. Your labor is not in vain (1 Corinthians 15:58). If not, pray that God would grant you the courage to start!

Again, if you need help, call your pastor. He is to be your servant in this effort. Allow him to work with you.

✠

TRINITY

More Than a Feeling

But the fruit of the Spirit is love, joy, peace, patience, kindness, goodness, faithfulness, gentleness, self-control; against such things there is no law.
—Galatians 5:22-23

How does that song go? *School's out for summer…*

Well, it's almost out. My kids have already said three or four times this morning, "Two and a half more days."

"Yes," I say in return. "You've already said that."

As much as I love education—just ask my wife, Jennifer, and she'll tell you I could sit in a classroom pretty much all day long— still, I'm glad the school year is coming to a close. It means time is a little more flexible for rest from busy schedules where every minute is accounted for, people's spirits seem much calmer, and perhaps the doors and windows of opportunities for more fellowship with one another begin to open. In all, the sky's deep blue feels just a little kindlier and the sun's rays seem somewhat more caressing.

You can't beat the feeling of summer. It can be very joyful.

In my morning reading from Luther, the good Doctor wrote the following regarding faith in Christ resulting in the joy of life and life's deeds:

> The better you know it, the more does it make your heart joyful, for where there is such knowledge the Holy Ghost cannot remain outside. And when He comes He makes the heart joyful, willing, and happy, so that it freely goes and gladly with good heart does all that is well-pleasing to God, and suffers what has to be suffered, and would gladly die. And the purer and greater the knowledge, the deeper grows the bliss and joy. (W.A. 12. 547.)

Do you know how Luther claims this joy is planted specifically—that is, the springtime sowing that produces the summertime image he just described? If you guessed Word and Sacrament—the Word of God and the Gospel preached, Baptism, Absolution, the Lord's Supper—then you're right. It's through the reception of these Gospel means that the perpetual summertime heart of the Christian is strengthened for real joy—come what may.

How does that song go? *More than a feeling...*

Faith in Christ results in so much more than a feeling. It results in life—a life lived together as a community of believers—caring for one another, opportunities to serve the needs of a suffering world, prayer, study of the Word, reception of the gifts of grace, and so many other things I could add.

Notice Luther connected joy to suffering and death.

Summer ends. Fall comes. A new school year begins, and with that, the schedules increase, and the days seem to get shorter. But the Christian heart fed by Christ's perpetual springtime love for a truly endless summer of joy knows this and is well stocked against anything that would try to steal it away.

Don't lose Word and Sacrament this summer. Don't stay away. Keep in holy worship. Be strengthened by the Means of Grace. They are your lifeline for joy—real joy—into and beyond the approaching summer.

☩

What Would You Do?

If possible, so far as it depends on you, live peaceably with all. —Romans 12:18

I'm going to go out on a limb and ask you a personal question, and it's one that, I suppose, could result in varying answers, and maybe even a few more questions. Who knows? Either way, I'll do what I can to parse it out.

So, here goes…

What would you do if you visited a church, and by chance, no one greeted you?

Now, think about your answer for a moment.

To unpack the question and put its contents a little more on display, let me tell you what I wouldn't do in such a situation.

First, unless someone met me at the door and was shouting at me and telling me I was unwanted, I wouldn't be so quick to assume that the church is unfriendly. That's far too big of an assumption to make of an entire collective of Christians who gather—with regularity—to receive Word and Sacrament for the forgiveness of sins, and for familial fellowship with others they know, love, and trust because they believe, teach, and confess the same things. And along those same lines, what does "unfriendly" mean, anyway? That's a loaded word these days. Speaking from experience, in the postmodern world in which we dwell, just about anything anyone says or does has the potential for being misinterpreted in ways that appear offensive and unfriendly, especially when it comes to theological things—Church things. For example, when I explain to some visitors from other denominations desiring to commune with us just why it is that the LCMS isn't in altar fellowship with their particular church body, I could stand there smiling, giving them crisp, clean 100 dollar bills, one after the other in cadence with every word, and they'd still tell me how unfriendly or unwelcoming I am and how our practice is offensive. No matter that the practice is written in the Word of God (1 Corinthians 10 and 11) and is even explained by Saint Paul as being to the benefit of all who approach the altar of God.

Just saying a church is unfriendly could be saying more about you than the church.

Do you know what else I probably wouldn't do? I wouldn't make an effort in the greeting line after worship to tell the pastor (and therefore the others around him listening) how unfriendly his church is in comparison to my own—unless, of course, my purpose was to make sure he knew about that guy calling me names and shouting at me when I first came in. But assuming that didn't happen, even if the church doesn't seem as peppy as your own, how does it help during a tranquil and joyous time following a worship service to passive-aggressively and bluntly point out what you are assuming are faults of the congregation? Even if you are right and the congregation isn't hopping over pews to greet you in the narthex or nave, offering you a cup of coffee and asking you out to lunch after the service, maybe it is for a very good reason. Maybe they're maintaining a level of reverence and devotion that is fast-fleeting in many other worship scenarios. Perhaps they are taking the words of Ecclesiastes 5:1-5 very seriously. But whatever the reason, an email—or better yet, a phone call—to the pastor later that day would be a better scenario for expressing the concern and then having the right amount of time and dialogue to dissect it—much better than the greeting line, that is. And God willing, the whole time the conversation with the pastor is occurring, it will be important to listen to his response carefully and to do your best to remember that he's the one man who probably knows the people of the parish much better than you ever will. He knows what's happening in their lives. He knows many of their secret sorrows. He knows their joys and the things that make them smile. He's seen them give of themselves to others without being asked. He's been in their presence when they've offered a kind word of support. His eyes have widened and his heart has melted away when they've called to get the address for someone they don't even know, someone who's struggling, so that they could send a gift card and note of prayerful encouragement. With all of this, he probably knows them to be some of the friendliest and most loving people he's ever met, and he probably loves them like family. Be ready to hear him express hurt when you try to tell him you see them as acting in deliberate unfriendliness. Listen for his genuine surprise. Be ready for him to defend them. And be ready to consider that you may be completely wrong about his church family.

Lastly, and personally, here's something else I probably wouldn't do. I probably wouldn't wait around to be greeted. This leads me now to what I would do, instead—and it's only one thing in particular.

I'd introduce myself to others.

In other words, I'd do my best to play my part in the fellowship of common humanity. I wouldn't work from the perspective of expecting others to take the first step toward me, but rather I'd do what I could to take the first step toward them. I know it isn't necessarily the easiest thing to do, but neither are a lot of things. With that, pray. Ask the Lord to give you the courage. And while you're at it, ask the Lord to cultivate the hearts of the people around you toward receptivity. Imagine if people just did these kinds of things instead of taking offense at others who didn't do what we really should be attempting to do ourselves. Still, even if I have to be the one to reach out, it would remain a grand connection between people, and quite possibly the beginning of a friendship God worked through an act of genuine Christian kindness.

In the end, I guess what I'm saying is: Who cares who greets who first? If you want to be greetable, be someone willing to step up and initiate the greeting, too.

Finally, and as a side note, once I meet and know someone in the congregation, I'm guessing that person will naturally become a helpful conduit for meeting others. If any assumptions are to be safely made, it's that a member of the congregation should be counted on to help their visiting friends make the necessary introductions. That seems to be a pretty organic expectation.

So, to conclude, I just thought I would share this with you. It's a little bit of practical analysis, and it isn't in any way meant to say that the people of any particular congregation are unfriendly. Most aren't! Concerning my congregation, I hear from nearly every visitor just how kindly the people are, and with that, I'm often walking on cloud nine knowing that I get to be a part of such a church family. Of course, there will always be those folks who miss the mark in grasping our identity, and with that, they'll say hurtful things—which again, in my opinion, reveal more about them than anything about us. Never mind that nonsense. Let the pastor handle it. Most of us are way past being slowed down by such simple things. Instead, rejoice in the knowledge that people are indeed coming in from the outside—people looking for substance—and they are discovering a Christian community that's seeking to be faithful to Christ and His Holy Word in all that they are—a congregation founded on Him, on His Word and Sacraments—the Gospel! Of course, in all of this, give all glory to God who, by His Holy Spirit, has made you His people and continues to strengthen you to be ones who are first to love and serve others rather than expecting them first to love and serve you!

✠

The Second Sunday after Trinity

You Are the Salt of the Earth

You are the salt of the earth, but if salt has lost its taste, how shall its saltiness be restored? —Matthew 5:13

On the way into the office this morning, I heard the newscaster suggest we're in for some pretty severe weather. He reported a flood watch in effect from 8 AM until 8 PM, so it would appear we're going to need to batten down the hatches and prepare.

Speaking of preparation, there's more readying to acknowledge when considering the following text from Matthew 5:13-16:

> (Jesus said) "You are the salt of the earth, but if salt has lost its taste, how shall its saltiness be restored? It is no longer good for anything except to be thrown out and trampled under people's feet. You are the light of the world. A city set on a hill cannot be hidden. Nor do people light a lamp and put it under a basket, but on a stand, and it gives light to all in the house. In the same way, let your light shine before others, so that they may see your good works and give glory to your Father who is in heaven."

Thinking on what the Word of God says here, it's hard to deny that we, the Christians, are often the means by which God blesses the world around us. In other words, He has prepared us for the work of being His own in visibly active ways.

I know, I know. It sort of sounds like I might start singing, *"They'll know we are Christians by our love..."* Don't worry. I won't. But still, there is a certain truth hovering within that old folksy song, and it is the possibility that as people look in from the outside, they'll see something different about us that could very well draw them to a particular end. That end being just as Christ says in the text: giving glory to the Father in heaven.

So, why does this matter? First, because if you are a Christian, this includes you. Second, because it is a precise encouragement for you to get in the game of life around you with the Gospel and to know that you are blessed as a servant of the One who fully intends to use your efforts in faithfulness, both in word and deed, to extend His kingdom to others in need for the sake of their salvation and His glory.

This truth in particular is foundational for the beginning of each day. It is a reminder that no matter what happens—that is, no matter how inadequate any of us may feel we are when it comes to proclaiming Christ as we go about our day, there's always the silent reality that exists even if only by our kindnesses through everyday words and deeds. In other words, you don't have to be a theologically eloquent superstar to shine the light of Christ in this world. Everyone has different gifts. But the gift that is common to all Christians is faith in the One who gave His life as the ransom for the world. This creates hope, and it draws us to a faithful expression of that hope to and for others in the world around us.

I pray this will inspire you for speaking the truth in love to others, not only by way of words, but also through the deeds of mercy, kindness, and benevolence.

✛

Showing Oneself to Be Teachable

If then you have been raised with Christ, seek the things that are above, where Christ is, seated at the right hand of God. Set your minds on things that are above, not on things that are on earth. —Colossians 3:1-2

As always, I want to try to give you something to chew on as you enter into the oncoming week, and the first thing that comes to mind is something that came up in the Adult Bible study yesterday.

At one point in the discussion, I mentioned Quintilian, a first-century Roman best known for his writings in the field of rhetoric. I don't remember the context in which this arose during the study, but the quotation I remember mentioning was:

> It is the duty of the master to teach. It is the duty of the student to show himself to be teachable.

That's an incredibly loaded bit of wisdom, and what it means, essentially, is that while a teacher should be apt and able to teach, it is just as important for the one listening to the teacher to do so with a certain level of humility and respect that displays a readiness and willingness to learn.

Quintilian isn't the first to suggest this. It was Jesus who brought a little child before the disciples in Matthew 18 and said that to be great in the Kingdom is to be like the little ones. One aspect of the Lord's intention at that moment was to point out the humble lowliness of a child. A humble person is a teachable person. A teachable person will know his or her own need and will seek to be led in truth.

It seems that more and more in this world—especially in the age of the internet—so many have been fooled into thinking they are experts on everything and anything. After a five-minute Google search on any particular topic, they feel comfortable in their internet-assembled position and equipped to challenge. I can tell you that no other field of employment on the planet experiences these challenges like the Office of Pastor. When it comes to theology, in a casual discussion at the local McDonald's, it becomes more about seizing the opportunity to tear down the clergy, showing them to be in error, than it is seeking after truth. In other words, more and more people are coming to situations ready to show themselves to be loftier in wisdom than the one called to stand in the front of the class. This is unfortunate, even in situations where the teacher may not seem to be all that substantive. For that, I'll give you an example.

Not all that long ago I was sitting among a group of pastors in Lansing who were chatting with a state representative. In the middle of the discussion, one of the pastors began what felt like a mini-sermon on a portion of Romans chapter 10. Now, remember, he was in a room full of pastors, so as you can expect, a good number of them tuned him out. I know this because the visual cues were more than apparent. I was tempted to do it, too. But in those situations, there's something I try my best to do. I listen intently to the information being given, listening for the pieces that I don't know as opposed to focusing on the general assumption that I've already mined the topic of everything it can offer. Not surprisingly, I noticed an angle to Saint Paul's text I'd never considered before. In other words, I learned something.

I suppose that perhaps one place I may be going with this as I type is simply to say two things. The first is that each member of every congregation always has a place as a student of the Bible. No Christian should ever feel as though he or she doesn't need to study it. More importantly, we should never believe that those called by Christ through His congregation to teach the Scriptures are somehow unworthy of our humble ear and attendance. Yes, again, the teacher must be substantive and well-prepared for teaching. The Scriptures declare this, too, and where it meets the Office of the Holy Ministry, hopefully, congregations are calling such men into their midst to be and do just that. But second, don't forget that the student has a role, too, and that is to show his or herself ready to be taught—present and attentive, listening and engaging in respectful back-and-forth discourse, not coming to the situation ready to hijack it and show how learned they are in comparison to the instructor, but rather ready to take what they know in stride with what they don't and then piece it together for the sake of, as Saint Paul encourages, reaching for the higher things and not settling for anything less (Colossians 3:1-2).

I pray this meets with your eyes and is received with a Godly heart. It's something that I do try to apply to myself. It's something that I hope you will, too.

✠

The Plans I Have for You

For I know the plans I have for you, declares the Lord, plans for welfare and not for evil, to give you a future and a hope. Then you will call upon me and come and pray to me, and I will hear you. You will seek me and find me, when you seek me with all your heart. —Jeremiah 29:11-13

This is a most pertinent text. It's one I know by heart, and perhaps you do, too. If you don't have it memorized, take a minute and cram it into your brain right now because it speaks an unmatchable word of truth from our God.

First, it is urging that believers understand that God has us in mind, and as Paul more or less repeats in Romans 8, the Lord's plans are for our benefit and never our harm. The hope that Jeremiah preaches as from God Himself, is salvation—redemption—victory over sin, death, and the devil through the life, death, and resurrection of the Messiah, Jesus Christ.

And so by faith, we call upon our God. We pray to Him and He hears us. We seek Him, and just as He has promised, we find Him in Jesus. To seek God with all our heart is to know by faith that in good times and bad, He is the shepherding deliverer.

I'm sure your congregation and her leadership, by the power of the Holy Spirit, have so wonderfully been living the essence of this text. And God continues to show you in so many ways that your trust in Him is not misplaced. When the temptation arises amid a financial challenge to revert to gimmicks or to attempt spending practices that are sure to seal a dreadful fate in unfaithfulness, God's people have turned to the Him and His Word, and it is there that they have found a secure footing every time—and remarkably, the storm clouds have passed and the sun has dried up the rain-like teardrops of fear.

God is so good. He has plans for you. He knows them. And they are for your benefit and for the good of those He desires to save through the Gospel efforts of your congregation.

From a pastor's perspective, thank you for knowing this. Thank you for being a faithful Christian who desires to live according to the Name placed upon you. Thank you for such diligence displayed by regular worship attendance, knowing that it is there you receive what is necessary for such a sturdy faith. Thank you for your willingness to serve in and around your church family's efforts— telling others about the joy you experience as a worshipping community, communicating the Gospel and encouraging people to join you, willingly and deliberately giving of your time and your talents to further the efforts of the Gospel-minded mission, and for supporting the hard work of both the paid and volunteer staff who serve tirelessly as the mortal cogs in an immortal machine.

God bless you. The people of my congregation mean the world to me. I'm sure you mean the world to your pastor, and that he thanks God for you every single day.

✝

Behold and See

See what kind of love the Father has given us, that we should be called children of God. —1 John 3:1

The Lord is with you this day!

Sitting and sipping my coffee this morning, I suddenly found myself recalling a moment with my friend and mentor, Reverend Dr. Jakob Heckert. He's with the Lord in the glories of heaven, now. Nevertheless, to remember him is to stir the familiar warmth of collegial togetherness and refreshment in Christ.

The moment that came to mind is one in which we talked about a great many things, one of which was the text of 1 John 3:1-3. We discussed verse one in particular.

In the original Greek text, the first word in the sentence is ἴδετε, which is typically translated as "see." Sometimes people will even translate it as "behold," although there's another word that's better translated as "behold." It's ἰδού. In particular, ἰδού is used when something extraordinary is happening—like an angel is delivering a message, or the Holy Spirit is descending on Christ at His Baptism. It is an emphatic word calling attention to detail or a particular idea. Another way to put it is that it is the "Wow, look at that!" of the first century.

But in 1 John 3:1, while the Apostle could have chosen to use ἰδού, he doesn't. It certainly would have been appropriate in the sense that being called a child of God is an amazingly incredible thing. But again, instead, he chose ἴδετε, a much simpler form which means to see something and understand—to comprehend its significance.

Jakob and I talked about this, and we realized that ἴδετε works well because the fuller context of the reading is specifically situated in Jesus Christ. In other words, certainly, we can marvel that we are God's children, but more importantly, we are to know and understand that the greatness of God's love—and therefore our role and title and His children—is seen and understood completely in the person and work of Jesus Christ, the One who died and rose again to win for us this blessed reality. The word ἰδοὺ draws attention to something you don't want to miss, but ἴδετε speaks to understanding what's at the heart of what is before you. In this case, it is the divine love of God displayed in Jesus on the cross for sinful humanity. Yes, even while we were God's enemies, He gave of Himself for our rescue. We see and understand this when we, by faith, look to His Son, Jesus.

This is all pretty wonderful.

And so, with that, look to the Son of God. See in Him God's undeserved kindness toward you. Looking upon the cross, know and understand the price for sin, but more importantly, look there to know and understand what Saint John calls ποταπὴν ἀγάπην—the sort of love (agape, which is the perfect love that only God can have) located in Jesus Christ.

Looking there, the Christian is never left to wonder about God's intentions for humanity. In Jesus, the message is crystal clear.

✠

Give Jesus to Your Children

For the promise is for you and for your children. —Acts 2:39

I don't know about you, but I sort of feel like the summer is already flying by far too quickly. It seems like only a few days ago we were getting ready for the last day of school. Time certainly does fly right by!

I know that in the days leading up to the break, my wife, Jennifer, and the kids put together a list of the extra things they wanted to try to do this summer—such as visits to the park, picnics, swimming, and a host of other things. The heat has been somewhat of an obstacle for several of the activities. My list involved doing a lot less than normal—in fact, a whole lot of nothing—and yet I've found myself in the middle of finishing a basement renovation before my eldest son Joshua's graduation party. It wasn't necessarily how I was planning to spend my midsummer evenings, but looking at it long-term, it will be worth the effort when it's done. I suppose there are a lot of things we can view from this same perspective.

Considering my son Joshua and looking back over the years, I'm sure that just like me, you can think of times when raising your children was a difficult task. You might even say it was one of the most challenging endeavors that the Lord ever allowed. It's not uncommon for Jennifer and me to turn at look at one another in any particular circumstance involving our children and say, "Would you have ever thought you'd be here right now?" The answer is almost always, "No." And it's an honest no, because when either of us was younger—still kids, in a sense—who'd have thought we'd ever find ourselves on the other end of the strange situations that we were

133

imposing on our own parents. Forget the diaper changes. That's not what I'm talking about. I'm talking about all-nighter in the Emergency Room because the child made a poor choice on the jungle gym, or terrifying diagnosis, or a conversation of comfort and encouragement in the face of a friend's harsh words, or the seemingly never-ending sanitizing when the Rotavirus is sweeping through the house, or sorting through a situation when the child did something wrong and found himself in trouble, or the countless hours of cleaning only to see everything wrecked again in less than ten minutes, or the arguments about this or that issue. I could go on and on, and I'm sure that most anything I'd share would resonate with many of you. But the point is that a lot goes into seeing a child through to adulthood, and while many of the events are not what we may have wanted or expected, I stand here at the edge of our first child's graduation from high school, and I say that the work was worth it.

But having said this, there's a more important point that needs to be shared, and it's simply that without the Lord and His Gospel at the heart of the effort, there'd have been no chance of true success. And by success, I don't mean that the child manages to stay out of prison and instead gets a great job, has a great marriage, and is a productive member of society. What I mean is that the child has been raised in a way to know the Savior, Jesus Christ, and the forgiveness of sins He has won by His life, death, and resurrection. This is most important.

I'm pretty sure I once shared in a sermon that while I've had many goals as a dad, the most important thing to me is that when I'm well situated in heaven's eternity, at some point along the way, my wife and children will be within arm's reach, and I'll be able to turn to them and say, "I'm so glad you're here." That's what I want most. And so all of the efforts now, no matter how challenging they may be, have as their primary strategy to keep Jesus in the middle of it all.

Always be willing to give Jesus to your children. And I encourage you to do this as much as you can while you can. Of course, this means being faithful in worship, but it also means keeping Christ at the center of life's occurrences—both good and bad. Again, things may or may not turn out for success in this life. Our children may stray. They may get into some serious, life-altering trouble. But in the end, their hearts will have been regularly cultivated to know that, ultimately, Christians are not inheritors of this world. We are inheritors of the world to come, and so we continue to introduce Christ to our families knowing that the Word of the Gospel is powerful, and in the hour of deepest need, there is the promise of forgiveness no matter how long and hard the road has been.

It will be a moment when the effort seemed so challenging—and sometimes even hopeless—but in the end, it will have been worth it.

I pray the Lord's blessings by this Gospel to you and your family. I am most certainly confident that it is the only true message of power that can change human history and establish the best future for our kids.

✠

Serving in the Church

Each of you should use whatever gift you have received to serve others, as faithful stewards of God's grace in its various forms. —1 Peter 4:10

As I write this, I'm sitting at gate A45 in McNamara Terminal at Detroit Metro Airport waiting for a flight to Louisville, Kentucky. I should probably be working on the sermon for this Sunday because I don't have very much of it completed. I only have a few paragraphs. The words have been somewhat elusive this week. I'm sure it will come to me. God is good that way.

In the meantime, I'm on my way to visit a congregation in Louisville, and it looks to be a promising time divided into two parts.

The overall effort will be to speak to a gathering of laypeople and pastors regarding Religious Liberty issues facing the Christian Church in America. For the first part, I'll be spending about an hour talking about the Two Kingdoms doctrine and taking questions. But then for the second part, we'll shift gears significantly. Knowing that I've authored a few volumes on whisky, the gathering's organizers have arranged for me to lead anyone who wants to stay for an extra-curricular whisky tasting.

What fun! Being smack dab in the middle of Bourbon country, I'm looking forward to the event.

This has stirred a thought.

As I sit here at gate A45 watching the masses pass by, I realize that while many are carrying various things—suitcases, children, you name it—the fact is that all are toting something invisible to the naked eye.

I'll bet you thought I was going to say "the sinful nature" or something like that. Well, I wasn't. And while you're right, the sin-nature is there, I was thinking of something else entirely.

Each person passing by, whether they realize it or not, is equipped with gifts they've been given by God. This reminds me of Saint Peter's words in 1 Peter 4:10.

Pondering this further, it carries me back to a conversation I had with the Principal of our day school a few days ago about certain things happening in our school—how we have so many wonderful volunteers serving in various capacities, all of whom make our Christian family a community and place of which we can be proud. But then as the conversation unfolded, we began to talk more about others in the parish who might have certain skills—gifts—that we could tap into for the sake of enhancing what we're already doing. For example, I suggested that I've long wanted to see our students have a space in the building—perhaps a corner of our library—that was made to look like a newsroom, and the kids would participate in weekly newscasts to the rest of the school. But among other things, this would mean finding funds, a volunteer coordinator, and some staging volunteers. I can think of quite a few students who would truly learn and shine by doing something like this, but of course, we'd need people with the right skills to help make it happen.

We also talked about topics like chess, quilting, and among other things, soap-making—all things that the kids might only have the opportunity to experience during special times like Lutheran Schools Week. I think we were both contemplating how these ideas might become more than that.

Now to bring the conversation back around to the people who are walking past me right now.

Maybe you're toting a special skill that you could share, something that would serve to enhance God's gracious care of the Christians in your community, something that will make their time together here in your Christian family that much more edifying. The folks I'm preparing to go and visit called upon me in a way that I might expect, but at the same time, they were keen on another facet of my personality and took a chance at asking if I'd be willing to share with them in a more light-hearted and fun sort of way. And of course, because it's something on the inside that I tote around to events like this, I was happy to oblige.

To conclude, if you can think of someone or some skill your pastor should know about—something that could be shared with your school's students and families as an extra-curricular effort—let the folks in charge know. Like me, I'm sure they want to continue to make their efforts in the Christian community the best they can be.

☩

Letting Her Go

Trust in the Lord with all your heart, and do not lean on your own understanding. —Proverbs 3:5

We just dropped our daughter, Evelyn, off at Camp Midicha, which is a week-long summer camp for kids with Type 1 diabetes. Needless to say, I am experiencing a strange mixture of emotions.

In one sense I'm terrified. And why? Because no one knows the particulars of her disease like her parents—not her doctors or her friends. Not even her siblings have it wrangled as we do. We know her numbers, and we know her physical cues. But we'll be offline for a week—unplugged from her care while others do the tending. In a way, this teeters at the edge of nightmarish.

In another sense, I'm so happy for her. I knew I could be when she, while sitting on my lap as we waited to register, leaned in and asked, "So, everyone here has Type 1?"

"They sure do, honey," I replied, kissing her cheek. "All of them. Even most of the counselors."

She sighed. "I'm not alone," was her priceless reply.

That's right, you're not. You're going to meet so many other kids who are fighting this monster just like you. And although it'll be lurking there the whole time, you're all going to have so much fun, and this will be like a collective punch to the fiend's face.

Lastly, I feel guilty. Why? Because as I said at the beginning of this little jaunt, Jennifer and I are now completely unplugged from the scene. In a sense, we get a break from the constancy of our daughter's care. But I don't want a break. She doesn't get a break, and so I don't want a break. It's with her day and night, and so I want it to be with me day and night. I want to carry as much of the load for her as I can. With that, there's guilt.

In the end, I know the experience will be a wonderful one for her. She's going to make a lot of friends and she's going to learn so much about how the other kids wrestle through it all, too. Who knows? Maybe by the time she gets home, she'll finally be convinced by a cabin mate that she really should try an insulin pump. Either way, I know the Lord will bless and keep her in His loving care. And when she comes home, we'll be here to scoop her up, hear all of her wonderful stories, and then continue together from where we left off, knowing that one day, in the realms of heaven, this stupid disease will be a thing of the past.

But again, until then, we're in this together and we'll keep going. Besides, God made Christian parents this way. He set us beside Himself as caretakers for His precious ones, no matter the context. This is one more reminder of His great love in this troubling world.

✠

In-Person

Therefore encourage one another and build one another up, just as you are doing. —1 Thessalonians 5:11

Y ou may recall from the introduction to this volume that everything you've been reading was written as it came to mind in the moment. In other words, the process is to ponder and type. As I do it, I pray that what results will be of use to the reader. Of course my ultimate goal each time is to, in some way, communicate God's Word. As these notes meet with the people I serve in Hartland, Michigan, when I'm done pondering, I go a bit further and report the regular news items of importance to the congregation.

Communication is key to so much, and it's worth every keystroke on this well-worn keyboard.

George Herbert, a Welsh poet, once said, "Good words are worth much, and cost little." I agree. Good words can be the difference between clarity and confusion, winning and losing, hope and despair, joy and terror.

In a certain sense, the Church deals in words. Of course, we know that our most precious vernacular, the Word of God, isn't just language. Rather, it is the very powerhouse asset that created the world and sustains us even now in the Christian faith. But as Christians with a sufficient understanding of the importance of God's Word, we're in a good place for observing how significant the actual structures and employment of language can be.

Words are important.

I think regular communication in a congregation has the potential for fostering sturdy relationships as well as building trust in the church's leadership (who, by the way, deserve to be trusted as they are faithful servants of Christ). I also think that it is a masterful tool for helping any congregation overcome obstacles, no matter what those obstacles might be. When the members of a congregation are talking to one another (and doing so regularly), they stand a better chance of successfully charting the landscape before them. They will be walking in stride and helping one another.

I suppose that another positive aspect of regular communication is that very little can surprise the congregation. And if something does surprise them, likely, they'll already be prepared to steer into it with a solution.

All of this speaks to the positives of communicating through a regular email message each week, and it makes digital communication, in general, seem worthwhile.

But having said all of this, I watched a quick YouTube video last night before bed which showed scenes of various people in different locales locked in stares with the screens of their computers and smart devices rather than in conversation with the person beside them. The point of the video was to show how we've lost the ability to communicate, and in so doing, we've forfeited our ability to make friends with other people. The funny thing is, even well before digital devices would ever be a sparkling glint life in the corner of a warming transistor, Charles Dickens wrote something rather prophetic in one of his shorter books entitled *The Wreck of the Golden Mary*. He offered:

> I have heard it broached that orders should be given in great new ships by electric telegraph. I admire machinery as much as any man, and am as thankful to it as any man can be for what it does for us. But, it will never be a substitute for the face of a man, with his soul in it, encouraging another man to be brave and true.

Indeed. I communicate with God's people in so many ways—through these writings, through phone calls, through texts, through social media—and yet I'll admit that no form of communication compares to the ability to sit beside a person, to see his or her face, to be stirred by the contours there that betray emotion, tone, and so many other things that God has woven into the fabric of what makes for humanity. It's really quite wonderful when you think about it, and as a pastor, it is one of the joys of everyday service.

In the end, I'm thankful that the people in my care take the time to read the messages I send. But also, I'm even more so thankful for the times I've been invited to sit together with them as friends, especially when those times have had as their goal the extension of Christ's kingdom.

Knowing the value of such in-person interaction, I encourage you to consider the next time you're sitting and reading something (maybe even this particular writing) while eating your lunch at the restaurant, waiting for your car at the repair shop, or wherever you may be, feel free to save it for later. Instead, say hello to the person next to you. And as you do, don't forget that as a Christian, you bear a language within you that can convince and convert the heart of your listener. It can stir a far better friendship—one with the Savior of the world!

"Season your speech," Saint Paul says. In other words, communicate the Gospel in conversation as the opportunities arise. I dare say those opportunities are all around us every day, and the best ones unfold in person.

✠

Outpacing the Sun

Do not worry about tomorrow, for tomorrow will worry about itself.
—Matthew 6:34

Well, summer is officially coming to an end and school will be starting very soon.

I've seen a few social media posts from various folks noting how they can't wait for their kids to get back to school. I've seen others from people with children who are dreading the return. They dread it because they enjoy having the kids at home all day. They enjoy the sights and sounds, as well as the more leisurely pace when it comes to obligatory things. I'd have to agree. And to be quite honest, the week leading into each new school year, I always get a little anxious. For one thing, I think this happens because my awake time has already begun to outpace the sun and I know that it'll be the same for the kids. What I mean is that for most of the year, I'm already awake and working well before the sun rises, and I'm still at it long after the sun has set. It isn't this way in the summer, and it's as if the sun knows it. Leading along with a gentler pace, there are times when the rising sun through our bedroom windows is the first thing I see when I open my eyes. And it is at the end of a reasonable day from the step of my front porch that I see the sun beaming a goodbye stream on the western horizon, telling me it's later than I think and urging me to bed, but also reminding me that it'll be sure to wake me when it's time.

It's when I think of the ramped-up and overly-busy schedules combined with the shorter days of fall and winter that I begin to get restless. I wonder how I'm going to do it all. Sometimes I find myself doing something that I'd be willing to bet you do, too. I begin segmenting my life into forward-looking timeframes. "Only forty-eight more days until All Saints Day," I'll say. Or perhaps I'll whisper, "Only fifty-five days until Christmas." I'll do this throughout the year, knowing that when I arrive at each particular point, I'm that much closer to a time when the pace will lessen and the sun will once again greet me in my bed rather than after the morning school bell.

But there's something else that hovers in the midst of all of this. No matter the time of year, it's always there. It's a short, caressing Word from Jesus in Matthew 6 to an anxious heart of worry:

> Do not worry about tomorrow, for tomorrow will worry about itself.

The Lord preached these words to a group of Christians—folks like you and me—living in the trenches of a life filled with plenty of things about which to be concerned. He preached them having already offered a powerful Gospel of love—a good Word that delivered into their hearts the message that He is their Savior, that He has them well in hand, and will never fail. And so when I hear these words echoing in my anxious skull, they almost always come out of my mouth in the way that Saint Paul enunciated them to the Church at Philippi: Do not be anxious about anything, but in everything, by prayer and supplication, with thanksgiving, present your requests to God. And the peace of God which surpasses all understanding will guard your hearts and your minds in Christ Jesus" (4:6-7).

Do you know what's happening here amid my worrisome state? The Holy Spirit is prodding my flesh and bones to know and acknowledge that I have a God who loves me. The proof is resident in the giving of His Son into death for my sins. He will carry me through both the times of leisure and the times of challenge.

I have nothing to fear. Period.

I pray for the same peace for you and your family, that God would give to you a tranquil heart whenever you find yourself facing an uneasy moment. Trust Him. He is sure to provide all that you require. And I dare say that in comparison to the fiery ball around which our planet spins day after day after day, there is a much better Son who has risen, and by this, His time among us never sets. He never disappears over the horizon. His face is always shining on us. And with that, no matter the time of year, we can go to bed in peace and awake again in the same joy we had when we closed our eyes.

✠

Nice Shirt

In all your ways acknowledge him, and he will make straight your paths.
—Proverbs 3:6

Well, today's a big day for my church and her day school. The students are back in the classrooms, the teachers are moving at top speed, and the world once again seems to be quickening its pace even as we continue to go forward together in the mercies of Christ.

Being together in the Lord means being able to share the details of our everyday lives. As the new school year's seriousness was being revealed, I was blessed with an opportunity to share with a friend an account of something that happened to me rather recently. I can share it with you. And as I know it will lighten the mood, maybe by the time the story is done, there'll be something of theological value to glean.

The story begins with a favorite t-shirt, one that I like to wear when I'm working around the house. It's one that my wife, Jennifer, bought for me at Walmart a few years back. It says "England" across the breast, and it has the Union Jack prominently displayed. I like the shirt. I like it a lot, and I happened to be wearing it one day while visiting the nearby Home Depot in search of wood screws and wall plates for some electrical outlets I intended to install in a basement storage closet.

I found the wood screws first, and then I made my way to the main aisle that would lead me to the section where I'd find the remainder of my required items. To get there, it was necessary to pass the appliance department. On approach, there was a rather rugged-looking fellow who appeared to be guarding multiple flatbeds, each bearing some larger appliances—things like dishwashers and microwave ovens. It was an impressive stash of items he was preparing to purchase. But even with his remarkable train of products, the man himself stood out as most notable in the collection. He was decked in red, white, and blue from top to bottom. Everything on him bore an American flag, from his bandana to his pants. Even his shoes testified to the pageantry. Admittedly, being the patriot that I am, I was impressed, and I felt almost as if I should remove my hat and put my hand over my heart as I passed him.

But I didn't, and that's because as I made my way toward him, I could more than tell that he'd locked onto me with a stare. Having forgotten what was on the t-shirt I was wearing, I didn't know why, at least not until he spoke.

"Nice shirt," he intoned sarcastically. I smiled and kept my passing pace. But then he added, "Ashamed of your country's flag, friend?"

Now, I suppose most folks would probably just have allowed the man his space and kept walking, relegating his rudeness to the obvious fact that he was more so zealous about the American flag than most. But still, I was a bit irritated, and I certainly didn't feel like explaining to him that I'm not ashamed of my country's flag. I love America. But I also love the freedom I have to wear my England t-shirt while working in and around my home. Still, what I did next, I suppose, could get me into trouble one day, and not just because I frequent this Home Depot fairly regularly, but because there's always that chance that this guy might wander into my congregation one day, and when he discovers me in the pulpit, things could get interesting pretty quickly.

Anyway, as immediately as he spoke, I turned and offered in my best British accent something like, "Oy, mate! It's 'ard enough I've to drive my motorcar on the wrong side o' the road, but must I also be coerced into 'splaining my shirt?!"

As you can probably guess, I didn't stick around long. Although, I stayed long enough to note that the surprise on his face was worth at least a couple of quid.

Returning to my previous pace, I continued my quest. I didn't want to continue the engagement because if I found myself drawn into an actual conversation, one in which I'd have to keep the charade alive, he would've eventually noticed that I can't keep the accent going for too long before it devolves into something more attuned to an Australian trying to sound Jamaican.

I can't say for sure, but I do think he tried to apologize as I walked away. I think he said something about respecting America's allies. Well, whatever. I turned the corner of the aisle I needed, grabbed my wall plates, and then took the long way back to the checkout lanes, traveling first among the ceiling fans and then through the outdoor garden department, all to evade my star-spangled antagonist and the possibility of being forced to betray my truest accent.

I suppose that in the end, the takeaways here could be a few different things. The first is that I'm just as normal as you when it comes to life in the world around us. (Well, sort of normal.) I get frustrated and respond in ways that I should try better to keep in check. The second is that we ought to be careful to impose our suppositions on others based solely on what we see. Everything you see may suggest validity in your comments, that is until the person opens his mouth to speak, and then you realize you were all wrong. I think this guy figured out rather quickly that he should be more careful about who he criticizes in public. Another could be that even when challenged, rather than challenging back in a way that has more than enough potential for backfiring, we can trust that we are free to be who we are in Christ and simply converse.

Looking back, I'm guessing because of my frustration, in a knee-jerk reaction to teach the guy a lesson, I missed a really good chance to not only share with him just how much I love my country and her flag, but I could have used that avenue of conversation to share with him the name of a wonderful church where he, too, could hear the Good News of the Gospel that, as Christians, we are free to enjoy in this nation.

I suppose there will be other opportunities in the future for getting this right. As I noted at the beginning, as God's people, we are cruising along in the mercies of Christ every day. With that, we can be assured that there will be. Also, we can be assured that we're well and good when these moments come along, and we are more than equipped to use them to the glory of Christ and the benefit of the neighbor.

✠

Surviving the Zombie Apocalypse

Though an army besiege me, my heart will not fear; though war break out against me, even then I will be confident. —Psalm 27:3

I was blessed to be visited by a brother pastor with whom I'm friends online but have never actually met in person. It was a pleasure to finally meet face to face.

At one point during the conversation, his eyes shifted to the shelf beyond my desk where I keep all of my classical literature volumes. If you've ever been in my office for any length of time, then you'll know I have a reasonably full assemblage of Dickens, Shakespeare, Twain, and so many others—all the good stuff. But as he was observing the selections from a short distance, he noticed lying sideways across the tops of editions by Hemingway, Hawthorne, and Poe a well-read volume entitled *The Zombie Survival Guide: Complete Protection from the Living Dead* by Max Brooks.

Yes, you read that rightly. I have a book that I read pretty regularly about how to survive a zombie apocalypse.

"What's a guy like you doing reading a book like that?" my friend commented.

The essentials of my answer: While the book is written with a tone of complete seriousness, it's easy to see how it deals with itself and its own momentousness as being nothing short of laughably entertaining. With that, it's not entirely uncommon for me, before wading into challenging moments of great seriousness, to first read from Psalm 27 or 32, and then to measure my own emotions by flipping through Brooks' volume for some satirical levity. In other words, after receiving the right comfort for my soul from the Lord, I'll say to myself before things get a little crazy, "Well, it could be worse," and then I'll turn to a chapter about how important it is in a zombie apocalypse to keep one's hair short lest the undead have one more thing to grab in close-quarters combat.

Yeah, I know. Silly, right? Still, I share it because it leads to a deeper point, at least for me—and I hope I can explain it properly. God speaks by way of His Word regarding the ultimate peace we have in Jesus, how it overcomes all things. This Word actually changes us to know that there is nothing that this world can throw at us that is so powerful that it can conquer our Lord and His promises. Giving this serious consideration, that's what I mean when I read the zombie guide and say, "Well, it could be worse." Sure, things can always get worse. Zombies are the perfect example. But still, the promise is that even if we suddenly find ourselves surrounded by them, the promises of God do not change. There's still nothing that can ever be so overwhelming in the life of a Christian that it can usurp God's loving might and His efforts to keep us steadfast in His Son, Jesus Christ.

Christ died that we might have eternal life—not a zombie-free life. With that in mind, and as silly as it may sound, I really can make my way into some pretty threatening situations without getting too flustered, overly-bothered, or angry. In fact, after reading about strategies for protecting a two-story home from a ghoulish horde, a smile and a lighter step comes a little more easily when talking to someone who'd much rather call me an enemy than a friend. And trust me, a kindly, easier smile in such circumstances is much more fruitful than one that is forced.

In the end, take what you can from this casual rambling by a fellow human being who struggles with sin and its challenges just as much as the next person. And I suppose you can be assured that if you ever need a good handbook on zombies, I'm your guy.

✛

What Crawls Underneath

I give them eternal life, and they will never perish, and no one will snatch them out of my hand. —John 10:28

Colette, the early twentieth-century French author, wrote in her book *Cheri* (which, by the way, I don't necessarily suggest you read):

> A door slamming makes one jump, but it doesn't make one afraid. What one fears is the serpent that crawls underneath it.

Now, even though I wouldn't endorse Colette's volume, I do appreciate the intention of the words, and here's why. They're meant to relay in a simple way that there are plenty of things capable of startling us in this life, things that cannot necessarily harm us. But we also know that sometimes there are things behind the door that can. What's often most terrifying are those things that get through the door even as we press ourselves against it trying to keep them out—things like illness, broken relationships, and so many other things that do indeed happen outside of our control.

I'm starting to think that the image of the snake slithering under the door is becoming the more common of the terrors we face in this life. So much in our lives and the world seem to be spinning furiously beyond our ability to keep up, and as a result, we feel like we're hanging on. But with that, I want to tell you what my friend Jakob tells me when I get to feeling that way—when I feel like I have too much to do and not enough time or energy to accomplish it all. (And by the way, I know when I get to feeling like this because I begin adding to my prayers a request for a cloning device so I can be in multiple places at once, as well as a teleportation device so that my clones can swiftly zip to these places and get their assigned tasks completed).

First, he reminds me that I don't have to keep up. God is in control. This brings to mind what Pope John Paul was once quoted as saying:

It's your Church, Lord. I'm going to bed.

Second, he reminds me that even as I may think I'm losing grip on Christ and His promises, the Lord is holding onto me with both hands—and His grip is the strongest. And lastly, he reminds me that quite often it's those times when I have no control over the situation that I learn to trust Christ more intently. And he's right. It's during those times when it seems like the situation couldn't get any more hopeless—that there doesn't seem to be a way out—that we see the life, death, and resurrection of Jesus Christ in all its glory as the ultimate deliverance from the terrors of this world. With this Gospel beaming in and through us, all terrible things behind the door—even the things that get through—have no footing for snatching us from the One who loves us enough to die in our place. In this, there's always hope.

Take this Gospel message into yourself today. Savor it. It gives life, and it's yours as one baptized into the death and resurrection of Jesus.

✝

I Couldn't Even Imagine It

Obey your leaders and submit to them, for they are keeping watch over your souls, as those who will have to give an account. Let them do this with joy and not with groaning, for that would be of no advantage to you.
—Hebrews 13:17

What a pleasure it was to have a visiting missionary and his family with us for worship and to lead the Bible study hour yesterday. To hear firsthand what is being accomplished by God's grace through such servants is incredibly heartening, to say the least.

There were two things in particular that he said yesterday that continue to resonate with me. The first of these is the story he told of a small gathering of people in Vietnam studying the Book of Concord. He noted during one particular visit with them, he expressed sadness to them that they were so terribly persecuted for their Christian faith. But one of the men in the group surprisingly replied that he hoped the persecution would never end. He explained that he was far more fearful that if the challenges ever subsided, the Christians might be tempted to begin taking what they have for granted.

This is an astoundingly potent truth, one that brings to mind the ever-present challenge of convincing American Christians not only why it is so important to be present in holy worship, but also to take the faith seriously—to know and understand that membership in the Church isn't just one freedom among many that we enjoy, but rather it is the design and desire of Jesus Christ for administering what you need to save your soul for eternal life. I would even go so far as to say that it is the single most important wellspring for the truest freedom that matters most in this world.

We seem to be losing this understanding in the American churches, and it brings to mind what I've heard from a former professor who spent some time in Madagascar. He said, essentially, that the Christians there consider the United States to be a slothful and ungodly nation, one that shows no concern for what faith in Christ really means, thereby making the U.S. a prime mission field.

Yes, Africa is sending missionaries to the United States. Who'd have ever imagined such a thing?

The other thing that came to mind during the presentation was the picture of his daughter holding her teacher's hand to her forehead. He explained that in Thailand when the students come into the classroom each morning, they are to exhibit a form of respect for the teacher by taking his or her hand and touching it to their foreheads. I researched this. It is a well-entrenched practice of culture. In one particular article, it noted that this was more a sign of reverence for the office of teacher, one in which the child acknowledged that he or she was not only well below the teacher in wisdom, but was willing to learn and be grateful for the lessons that would be placed into their minds by his or her hand.

Again, I wonder if, in the swelling tide of radical individualism in America, we are losing this fundamentality. To illustrate, consider the following.

Truth be told, it is becoming more and more common that I end up in conversations with students in our school who have shown a surprising level of disrespect to a teacher, whether it's blatant obstinacy or simply bad manners and discourteous speech. Roles are becoming blurry.

But no matter the behavior, even as the opportunity for repentance and forgiveness is fostered, in these moments I've found it necessary to make one thing very clear as I'm speaking to the child: No student in the school is my equal, and no student in the school should consider his or herself to be equal to any of the adults on the premises. Certainly, a student may be counted as an equal at home or by a coach on a team or whatever, but here in the order of academia, the child is the child and the adult is the adult, the student is the student and the teacher is the teacher. Proper adherence to this order as it is born from the Fourth Commandment is expected, and when it is time for it to be enforced, if there is an unwillingness to comply, there should be the expectation of unpleasant proceedings.

I dare say that there was a time when all of this, for the most part, was innately understood in classrooms. But not so much anymore. We have to teach this now. What I mean is that as a young student, it would never even have crossed my mind to show up for class having deliberately disregarded my homework assignment just because I didn't want to do it. Likewise, it never would have crossed my mind to be told by my teacher to do something and to so plainly tell them, "No, I'm not going to do that."

I could never have imagined it then. As the pastor of a school who is familiar enough even with the educational philosophies in the public schools, I can see that the problem is fairly inescapable in our nation.

Now, before I leave you with the impression that I came away from the presentation completely deflated, you should know that I didn't. Instead, I was reinvigorated by the joy of knowing that in so many places across the world—in fact wherever the Gospel is being preached—it is being sponged by the people. God is at work and people are being brought to faith. As a result, there is a genuine craving for pastors, teachers, Bibles, hymnals, the liturgy, and so many substantive things that make for and sustain faith in Jesus Christ. This is exciting to see, and I know that a congregation like ours understands the crucial nature of such mission work and we want to see it continue. It's one reason why we continue the fight to maintain confessional Lutheranism in this place and we will never bow to surrender the importance of preserving a Christian day school in our community. It is well worth the struggle.

Praise God for this power of the Holy Spirit by the Gospel among us! Let it be the lens for interpreting the challenges that are ever before a gathering of Christians, while at the same time stirring us to know that no matter how tough things may be, our labor in the Lord is never in vain!

☩

A Love Like Theirs

Let love be genuine. —Romans 12:9

I have a story to tell you about Wally and Ellie. The Christians in my congregation would know them. When they were able to be in worship, they'd sit together on the pulpit side of the nave near the front. Technically they're not members of the congregation, although as lifelong and faithful Lutherans, I treated them as though they were. They'd been attending for some time thanks to one of our families stopping by and picking them up. Although that came to an end this past year when Ellie suffered a mild stroke and became homebound.

Still, I have a story to share, and because I'm a storyteller at heart, I thought I'd do it in narrative form. I hope you'll take the time to read it. I share it as I beheld it in my mind's eye while Ellie shared it with me.

It was the Fourth of July. It had been a long and tiring day. Even so, neither complained. The time with their son and his children was precious and always well worth the toll to the body.

Wally unlocked and opened the door to the apartment, being sure to turn on the light while at the same time holding the door for Ellie, just as he always did.

"Thank you, dear," she said, moving slowly with her walker. Once inside, she made her way to her favorite recliner, which was just beyond their little round kitchen table stacked with various knickknacks held sacred by both. Giving as full an exhale as her petite frame could, she plopped down and closed her eyes.

Wally followed. Placing his hand on her tiny shoulder as he passed, he offered, "It's getting late, Ellie." Mirroring his frail bride, he dropped into his favorite place on the couch just across the way from her. "How about we do our devotion and then get to bed?" he asked.

"Okay," she whispered, her eyes still closed.

Wally reached to the coffee table at his knees, and taking a volume from the top of a short stack of tattered editions, he turned to a page already being reserved by a frilly bookmark Ellie had made in a former day, a time when her eyes and hands kept a keener pace.

He read the text—a brief portion from John 6 describing a faltering crowd of Jesus' followers and Peter's words of faith, "Lord, to whom shall we go? You have the words of eternal life." A simple explanation by the devotional's author followed. In all, it only took a few minutes. Ellie closed with prayer. She gave thanks for the wonderful day with her husband and family. They prayed the Lord's Prayer together.

"Ok, then," Wally said, closing the book and returning it to its place. "I'll close up out here. You go on ahead and I'll be there in a minute." His back quite sore from the day, he gave a slight grunt and arose to help Ellie. Repositioning her walker, he took her hand into his and helped her to her feet.

"I'll see you in a minute," he said again.

"Ok," she said softly. "Don't be long."

"I won't."

Ellie was already in bed when Wally came in. He changed into his pajamas and climbed in beside her. But he was only there a moment before pulling back the covers and getting out of bed.

"I'm feeling a little warm," he said. "I'm going to go turn the air down a bit." Another moment passed and he was back. Ellie turned toward him as he worked to fluff his pillow.

"I love you," she said.

"I love you, too," he returned.

They kissed.

Ellie reached to turn off the light, and with its click, she settled back in beside her husband. A minute or two of silence between them, Ellie offered a final remark for the evening. "It certainly was a wonderful day," she said. "A truly wonderful day."

Wally didn't answer.

"Are you already asleep?" she chuckled wearily, turning back toward him in the darkness. Wally was silent.

She nudged him once. And then again. Turning back to the bedside table, she turned on the light. Wally's eyes were closed, but his mouth was open. She nudged him again, and this time he gave a gurgling sound. He wasn't sleeping. He was struggling.

She called the emergency number for the facility, and within minutes a team was in the apartment attending to Wally. In Ellie's own words, from that moment until the time they arrived at the hospital, life had become somewhat blurry. She doesn't remember getting dressed. She doesn't remember the drive. She remembers being gathered at his bedside and hearing the doctors say that Wally had suffered a massive stroke and that his time with her would most likely be very short.

Ellie stayed with Wally through the night.

Their son arrived the next morning, bringing in tow his eight-year-old daughter. Wally was showing signs of consciousness— holding Ellie's hand and squeezing when she asked him questions, affirming for her that he trusted in Jesus for his salvation, and smiling whenever she talked, even if it wasn't to him. He loved her voice. He had always loved her voice.

In the hushed hospital room, somehow Wally became aware that his granddaughter had brought along a pen.

"Grampa's wiggling his fingers to me, Grandma," the little girl said.

"I think he wants your pen, honey," she replied. Without hesitation, the little girl placed the pen into the hand of the man she'd so often given her own hand to hold. But there was no paper, and so Ellie turned over an empty tissue box to its plain white base and gave it to her granddaughter. The little girl held it firmly. Wally wrote in large capital letters.

LOVE ELLIE, he crafted slowly and carefully.

"He loves you, Grandma," the little girl said as Wally continued scribing something else, a number.

"71?" the eight-year-old asked, turning back to her grandmother.

"Seventy-one years," she said, her mouth betraying a quiver and her eyes beginning to wet. "We've been married for seventy-one years. That's how long we've been together. That's how long he's loved me."

Adorned with a toothy smile, "Write something for me, Grampa," the cheerful grandchild said.

Giving a labored but still genuine smile to match hers, he reached to the tissue box and began to scribble again.

S... O... M... E... T... H... I... N... G.

Ellie, her son, and her granddaughter beamed brightly together.

"He wrote you 'something,'" Ellie said and grasped for Wally's hand.

He took his last breath at that moment.

This is the story as Ellie recalled it while we sat together last Tuesday. Again, as you can see, I took the liberty of crafting what I was visualizing as she spoke. It was a Godly and serene event, one in which Ellie, even now, takes great comfort.

"Wally is with Jesus," she said. "And I don't feel slighted at all. We had 71 years together in a wonderful, Christian marriage."

"This is true, Ellie," I said. "And thanks be to God, because of Jesus, you'll see him again."

"Yes, I will," she replied. "I'll see him again. Who knows when that'll be, but I know it'll be."

Wally is with Jesus. By the power of the Holy Spirit, Ellie is at peace in this wrestling with death. The Gospel wins.

On the way back to the church, my car radio was tuned to a local rock station. Normally I have it on a talk radio station, but for some reason, today was different. Still thinking about what had just happened, I adjusted the volume much lower than it was when I arrived. It just felt wrong to listen to anything other than silence. Still, I could hear a familiar voice through the speakers. True to the station's ordinary playlists, it was Axle Rose, the lead singer of Guns N' Roses, and he was singing a familiar song from the late 80s, one that spoke of his pride in his ability to bed pretty much any woman he wanted, capped by nights of heavy drinking that turned into half-conscious days of gritty debauchery. It was a song that described the absolute opposite of what I'd just heard and seen.

Now, I don't know anything about Axle Rose. I don't know his beliefs, and even if I did, I could never tell you the contents of his heart. Nevertheless, in that moment of contrasting images, I imagined that if his lyrics are in any way revelatory of the truest corners of his viscera, like the rest of us—like Wally—he will one day breathe his last, and when he does, I wondered if he'd ever be able to scratch on the bottom of a tissue box for someone else what Wally scratched for Ellie. Would he even have an Ellie, someone there holding his hand, being with him through the darkest hours of the night, reminding him of Jesus, encouraging him to trust in the One who breaks the darkness?

I wondered.

But then I thought of something else, and I sat in my car in the church parking lot for a few minutes savoring the realization.

For one, seventy-one years is a long time to be married, especially in this day and age. It's something to be celebrated. But seventy-one years is also a time frame in which plenty of struggle is possible. I know this to be true. Wally and Ellie told me the stories of their lives when I visited with them. Just for starters, I know they lost three children to cancer, each at a young age. Such things can tax a marriage to its extremities and has the potential for causing divisions between a husband and wife that many of us will never fully know.

In one sense, and looking on from the story I shared, they had a perfect marriage. But we all know that no marriage is perfect and that's because no human is perfect. You, me, Axle Rose, Wally, and Ellie, we all swim together in the fellowship of human depravity and require help from outside of our sphere. This means that while some marriages will last seventy-one years, others will only last six months. This means that some will be able to live their lives without fear of addiction while others won't, and yet, all will have grievous thorns in their flesh that haunt just the same and bear an equal potency for separation from God.

We're in this together. That's our first point of order. But the overarching lesson to be learned is not necessarily that Wally and Ellie had a Maybury life in comparison to a guy like Axle Rose, but rather it is that together they were a living testament to the fact that Jesus was there, right in the middle of it all, proving that His Gospel is powerful enough to outlast the assaults, temptations, and storms that came to them throughout the seventy-one years. The moments at the end of Wally's life are a collage of images declaring this. It is for us to look upon them and be moved to know that Jesus is right in the middle of it all for us, too, no matter what we're experiencing.

In all truth, we already know that He's the kind of Savior who goes right into the midst of the messes, who'll sit down right next to Axle Rose and dine with him, giving the same Gospel that can convert and convince for faith. Certainly, He's dining with you and me, too. In humility and faith, we're willing to acknowledge that we're at the table with the tax collectors and sinners.

So, to bring this to an end, I suppose the first thing I'd encourage among you is to rejoice in the blessings God has given to you, namely that He has granted you faith in Jesus. But rejoice also that He has so generously sustained you and your family in the middle of a world that is most certainly coming undone. Second, give thanks that whether or not He has allowed an "Ellie" of sorts in your life or immediate family, you are surrounded by a congregation of believers, a fellowship of saints, who love you, pray for you, and would most certainly be there at your bedside if your last hour was at hand. Why? Because we know we're in this together. We're God's family. Third, and perhaps last, think on those who don't know such peaceful joy in this life. Prayerfully consider how you might take this peace that you have here among your Christian family and communicate just what it means to you while in the presence of others drowning in an often overwhelming tide of secularism. There may be an Axle Rose or two who realize contentment in this life is much more than money, possessions, and a life of self-service; and maybe through your Gospel words and actions, they'll see the Lord Jesus sitting at the table with them and giving to them something so much better.

✠

Visiting with the Classics

Let your speech always be gracious, seasoned with salt, so that you may know how you ought to answer each person. —Colossians 4:6

For me, as a pastor—as a man who pretty much writes a five-page paper each week and needs time to refill his mental reservoir in various ways in order to do it—not only have I had the chance to really dig into the Word of God, but at the same time, I've managed to visit a little here and there with some of the finer bits of literature from folks like Twain and Dickens.

I like these two writers immensely. Twain cultivates insightful observation. Dickens is an artisan of language.

It may sound somewhat trite to say, but the classics are classics for a reason. They have a proven way with words. They communicate so well, and in this, they have become tools for teaching communication. I think they are gifts to preachers. They emulate ways we might use language for introducing a listener to Jesus.

I know, I know. Someone might already be thinking, "Just preach the text, Thoma, and don't worry about this kind of stuff." To that, I say, "Humbug." I say this not because I don't want to preach the text. What I mean is that when you intentionally employ some of the communication tools—things like point-of-view, simile, hyperbole, personification, and others—you find yourself capable of communicating in a way that's less talking *about* Jesus and more preaching Jesus to the listener. In other words, and by way of example, let's say you want your son to meet the new child who just moved in down the street. You could tell your son about him, or

167

you could put in the extra, more intense effort and walk him down there and introduce him. With this, you've made your son a participant in the event, and in so doing have cultivated a better soil for friendship.

Care with the language that goes into the sermon—looking at all of the appointed propers, hymns, and the like, and finding ways to join them all together with a verbal cadence set on true faithfulness—well, this takes work. But in the end, it's well worth it. Additionally, and personally, I think it helps to keep the never-ending task of preaching the same texts over and over again somewhat fresh. And I suppose that in a purely human sense, it helps the listener absorb and maintain what's been preached for a little longer than five minutes.

Of course, preachers can safely admit that in all of this, the Holy Spirit will impact the heart exactly how He sees fit when the Gospel is purely preached. Still, that should never give the preacher license to be lazy with the task and ultimately the words. He's not putting on a show, but he is doing everything he can to handle the Word of God carefully and to communicate it the best way.

I think that visiting with the classics helps in this effort, and so I do it. And I suppose no matter your station in the Church, when it comes to communicating the Gospel to others, you might consider doing it, too.

☩

The Seventeenth Sunday after Trinity

Immersed in What You Love

Blessed are those who hear the Word of God and keep it. —Luke 11:28

During a recent Bible study, I mentioned to the participants that because I'd spent a good portion of the previous week trying to adjust to a new medication, I didn't actually get to the meat of a recent sermon's writing process until very early in the morning on the day it was to be preached. That happens far more than I'd prefer, and when it does, I don't like it.

I don't like it because I don't feel as prepared with the text, at least not as prepared as I think a preacher should be. Still, I used the time I had at my disposal, and I kept close to a simpler pace of just observing the scene in the text and then being what I am as a Christian man—someone who is excited to know Christ, a witness who wants to tell you what I've seen and heard, a friend who wants very much to introduce you to Jesus. Working from this perspective, the task of preaching is rather eventual. It has a way of coming alive. It has a way of becoming otherworldly and beautiful, and it has the potential for causing anyone to feel a little like Andrew running to tell his brother Peter, or Philip running to tell Nathaniel, "I have found the Messiah!"

But this reminds me of something else, too, and a guy by the name of O.C. Edwards poked at it when he wrote:

> When you come right down to it, the idea that the most exciting message the world has ever heard can be presented in a way that makes it sound old hat and dull is mind-boggling. There are probably only two circumstances under which that could happen. First, we are uninteresting, or second, we find the gospel uninteresting. In either case, something ought to be done about it.

169

Truth be told, he's talking about those who are called to preach. Nevertheless, I think his words still resonate for all Christians in a practical way, especially as the Church finds herself more and more immersed in a culture of religiosity where the Gospel is just one thing among many things, and often considered as not all that important in comparison. To say it another way, Christians are not immune to portraying to the world that we like the Gospel, but we don't necessarily love it. When this is true, it affects the way we communicate Christ to others.

Maybe another, more practical way to think about this would be to consider something that Richard Hays, a New Testament professor at Duke Divinity School, once said about one of his former professors, Alvin Kernan:

> When I was an undergraduate at Yale University, students flocked to Alvin Kernan's lecture courses on Shakespeare... Even though it was the late 1960s and we were living in an atmosphere charged with political suspicion and protest, none of this overtly impinged on Kernan's lectures. Kernan was not a flashy lecturer. What, then, was the draw? He loved the texts.

In other words, Kernan was an expert on Shakespeare, but being an expert didn't make him a productive communicator of Shakespeare. Hays sheds a little more light:

> His teaching method, as I remember it, was simply to engage in reflective close readings... delineating their rich texture of image and metaphor and opening up their complex themes – moral, philosophical, and religious. Often, Kernan would devote a significant part of his lecture time to reading the text aloud, not in a highly dramatic manner, but with sensitivity to the texts' rhythms and semantic nuances. I would often sit in class thinking, "Oh, I hadn't heard that in the text before." And I would leave the class pondering the problems that Shakespeare addressed: love, betrayal, fidelity, sacrifice, death, and hope.

Quite simply, Kernan was in love with and devoted to the texts of Shakespeare. When he wasn't teaching Shakespeare, he was reading Shakespeare and enjoying it for himself, and this directly affected his telling of the story to others.

Jesus said, "Blessed are those who hear the Word of God and keep it" (Luke 11:28). I'm sure I've shared with you before that the word Jesus uses in the Greek for "keep" is one that relays a defense of something considered to be invaluable to its owner. Considering this, while at the same time knowing that by faith, a Christian is in the deepest of love with the One who spoke the words, we learn something very important.

And here's where I'm going to suggest that you follow Kernan's example and immerse yourself in the study of something you love.

If you aren't in one already, consider joining a Bible study in your church. I say this because the regular study of the Word of God is crucial!

Now, don't stop reading here. Keep going.

Through the study of God's Word, not only is the Christian fed from the divine wellspring that gives true wisdom for salvation, but there's another product of the effort that many might overlook, and it's that it provides a depth for a multitude of discussions. And when one is truly prepared, one is much more confident and convincing. Again, what I mean is that there's a genuine difference between someone who knows *about* the Ark of the Covenant and someone who has spent time in the Word admiring its golden dimensions. There's a difference between someone who knows *about* the Israelites being pursued by Pharaoh and someone who, through the deliberate study of God's Word, has had the opportunity to be led in a way that sees the fear in the Israelites' eyes and feels the quaking ground—the rocks trembling and the dust rising as Pharaoh's army charges toward them in pursuit. There's a difference between knowing the story of the feeding of the five thousand and being so aware of the implications of the event that one can begin to hear the rumbling stomachs of the hungry crowd and be concerned. It's one thing to say so nonchalantly, "Yeah, Jesus died on the cross," but it's something altogether different to study Saint Paul's words regarding the depth of the event, and by this, to be led to envision the blackened clouds of darkness and to feel the stern breezes casing the scene at Golgotha. I could go on and on, telling you how Easter is just one thing that happens every year for so many Christians, and yet for those immersed in the study of God's Word, it is an emotionally jostling celebration that sees the absolute unexpected become reality—sin and death have been done away with forever— and it's a reality that applies to us right now!

As I said, I could go on and on about these things. Why? Because I love sharing them. With that, I pray that you'll take these words to heart and you'll think about joining a Bible study. My words are given here in love as they are given from someone who, like Andrew and Philip, has met the Messiah and truly wants for you to meet Him, too.

☩

De Morte

In the midst of life we are in death.   —Luther's Antiphon

Type 1 diabetes is a terrible disease. My daughter has it, and I truly despise it. My cousin, Rick, had it. He died this morning. He was 47.

In his youth, a stocky comrade, he was someone you'd want on your team when the neighborhood kids got together for a game of football. Flag football? No, that was for the weak. We were out for blood. And Ricky, when he had the ball, was pretty much a juggernaut. On more than one occasion, it took both me and my brother Michael to take him down, and that was only after he'd dragged us twenty yards.

Back in the day, no one used the term ADHD. There was no such thing. But if someone ever used the words "hyperactive," Ricky came to mind. In fact, at some point along the way he'd been coached by someone to vigorously shake his hands when he could feel the energy building, except as he did this, it was less of a tool of release for him and more of an indicator that we'd all better get the heck out of his way. For those of us on his team, that was the moment you knew to hand him the football.

Ricky was a counterpart to so many of the adventures of my childhood—camping trips, late-night gatherings with family and friends, endless biking around Danville, Illinois where we grew up. You name it, Ricky was often there somewhere. He didn't have siblings. We were his siblings. His dad left when he was very little, and so we filled that void, too.

He also didn't have a pancreas that worked the way it was supposed to. Like my daughter, Evelyn, his Type 1 diabetes was pretty much the center of his gravity. As a kid, I didn't necessarily know the breadth of the disease my aunt would refer to when giving him a shot, but I knew it was there. It was the only thing that ever seemed to bring Ricky, the powerhouse kid on the team, to a halt.

I never really fathomed the seriousness of his plight.

Even as he grew older and we lost touch, having lived so far away from one another, I wasn't kept unaware that his body had begun to succumb to the darker prospects of the disease. A few limbs were amputated and eventually, he went blind.

As I said, he died last night. Complications from Type 1 diabetes is what will be printed on the certificate.

Having said all of this, it wasn't all that long ago that someone said to me that there are so many children out there who have it far worse than my daughter. In that moment, I was angry about the statement. Of course, I know it's true. Things could be worse. But still, it was a heartlessly ignorant thing to say. In a sense, I've held onto that ignorant lack of understanding of this disease, and I suppose it was for a moment like this.

Yes, we Christians know that no one knows the day or hour of one's death. Only the Lord knows these things. It could be fifty years from now. It could be tomorrow. But there is a statistical "normal" we have as humans, and the terrible truth is that people with Type 1 diabetes, on average, live much shorter lives than those whose pancreases are intact. To be specific, they live an average of sixteen to twenty fewer years than others.

In this situation, Ricky lived thirty years less than a man my age probably will, and as you might expect, this is a terror that lurks in the minds of parents of Type 1 children.

But I trust Christ. I know my daughter does, too. Still, when I look at her, this little bit of ungodly information twists my insides in ways that result in the feeling of needing to micromanage the little things. I know my wife, Jennifer, feels the same way.

With that, I'm not sure what to say from all of this. I suppose I could offer that if you know the parent of a Type 1 diabetic, know also that there are hidden concerns that might cause them to seem overly dramatic. Don't tell them it could be worse. They already know it, and the hovering they do above their children is the evidence. They already know that while they're in charge of the care, every little bit of micromanaged success in the fight against this monster means a changing of the odds. To me, it means that for as long as I can, I'm going to work to make sure my little girl has a better shot at outliving me and not the other way around.

But as I already said, I trust Christ. I know His will is best, and that brings peace even in the midst of death.

✛

I Think It's Warm in Pasadena

See that you do not despise one of these little ones. For I tell you that in heaven their angels always see the face of my Father who is in heaven.
—Matthew 18:10

I want to share a quick fabric of thoughts that came to mind during a conversation with three of my four children while walking into the church one morning before school. It started when my son, Harrisons said somewhat randomly, "I wish we lived in Pasadena."

"Why Pasadena?" I asked.

"Because I think it's always warm there," he answered.

"You don't even know where Pasadena is, Harrison," his youngest sister, Evelyn, chimed in a less-than-helpful way. "For all you know, it's in Antarctica. Pasadena is prob'ly full of penguins."

This particular interaction recalled for me another interaction between Evelyn and Harrison this past Monday at a park near our home. I posted the conversation details on Facebook soon after it happened. Here's what I wrote:

> "Harrison!" Evelyn shouts across the public playground filled with families. "I need to ask you something really super important!"
> "What?!" her brother replies loudly, sounding annoyed.
> "When the zombie apocalypse comes, where do you think it'll start?"
> That's my girl.

Now the first reason I'm sharing these two stories with you is that, as the adage relays, kids say the darndest things, and with that, I just wanted to share them with you—my friends. Second, because it is once again a reminder of the depth that children possess. If you are listening to them when they are speaking, you'll hear (and perhaps even see) a different perspective on the intricacies of life in general. You'll find yourself being ushered through a portal into a completely different sphere of reality that is both complex and simple all at the same time. It's rather fascinating. And third, if you are thinking Biblically, it feeds into the reasons that Jesus instructs as He does in Matthew 18:1-6, 10.

> At that time the disciples came to Jesus, saying, "Who is the greatest in the kingdom of heaven?" And calling to him a child, he put him in the midst of them and said, "Truly, I say to you, unless you turn and become like children, you will never enter the kingdom of heaven. Whoever humbles himself like this child is the greatest in the kingdom of heaven. "Whoever receives one such child in my name receives me, but whoever causes one of these little ones who believe in me to sin, it would be better for him to have a great millstone fastened around his neck and to be drowned in the depth of the sea... See that you do not despise one of these little ones. For I tell you that in heaven their angels always see the face of my Father who is in heaven.

Jesus pointed to a simple humility and trust found in children that is iconic of saving faith in the Savior. He wants adults to have it. Such faith lets itself be led. It speaks the contours of its truth unhindered by shame. It longs to be with the One who is its greatest love, and it's sad in its deepest corners when there is separation.

But there's more He wants us to know, even as it meets children right where they are.

Again, children let themselves be led. They have no problem saying what's on their minds. They grow to love most deeply that which is set before them as most important, and they learn to despise the things that aren't. Parents are the ones setting the pace in these regards.

Notice also how the Lord offers a stern warning to those who would get between children and Himself. He doesn't mince words.

He says that anyone who causes one of the little ones to sin—that is, makes it so that they are led into a life of separation from Jesus, taught to love being away from Him, trained to despise His Word, shaped to see time with Him as one option among many valuable opportunities, molded toward a coldness for the Christian life— Jesus says it will be easier to swim with a two-ton millstone on your neck than to stand against the judgment at the Last Day.

As you can see, He takes this very seriously. As parents, as families together, as a congregation, we do, too. I know that when I observe my children—when I hear them say the crazy things that they say and when I see them do the even crazier and yet inspiring things that they do—I couldn't imagine keeping such gems of God's creative act away from the One who made them who they are. I couldn't imagine sleeping in on a Sunday morning and skipping worship—not even once! I belong there. They belong there, too. In fact, according to the Lord's bidding, this belonging is the point of reference for adults. It is something to which we look for direction, not the other way around. He said we must be like them when it comes to this humble desire and trust. I think Oskar Pank observed it best. I added the following quotation from Pank to the "Afterword" portion of my book *Type One Confessional*. He wrote:

> As the flower in the garden stretches toward the light of the sun, so there is in the child a mysterious inclination toward the eternal light. Have you ever noticed this mysterious thing that when you tell the smallest child about God, it never asks with strangeness and wonder, "What or who is God—I have never seen Him," but listens with shining face to the words as though they were soft loving sounds from the land of home. Or when you teach a child to fold its little hands in prayer that it does this as though it were a matter of course, as if there were opening for it that world of which it had been dreaming with longing and anticipation. Or tell them, these little ones, the stories of the Savior, show them the pictures with scenes and personages of the Bible—how their pure eyes shine, how their little hearts beat!

True. All true.

For any reader with children, as the new school year comes into view, take these words into yourself and consider them. As parents, be diligent in getting your kids to church. As observing grandparents, congregation members, and friends, consider what you can do to encourage the parents in the pews to keep at it. What can you do to show that you are rooting for them? How can you help in what can sometimes be a struggle with antsy little ones? Maybe all it would take to help the dust of frustration settle a bit would be a smile and a word of encouragement. Maybe a pat on the back and a "Keep at it, mom. You're doing the right thing" is all they'd need.

✠

Forgiveness in Stride

And forgive us our debts, as we also have forgiven our debtors.
—Matthew 6:12

I had a conversation just before worship one day about the joys of email. I and my counterpart were in agreement that sifting through thirty or forty each morning, trying to prioritize and then respond to them, is just not one of life's mesmerizing beauties. Don't get me wrong. I love the messages I receive from folks. The trouble comes when I miss one that is important or I get my prioritizing wrong and I don't respond to something as quickly as I should.

I struggle with those kinds of things, sometimes. In fact, it happened fairly recently. I received an email from one of the co-chairs of the Board of Trustees, and in it, he shared some pretty important things about the facility's current and future needs. Well, guess what? The email got lost in the shuffle and I missed it completely. There it sat for over a week. With that, you can imagine my embarrassment when he asked me if I'd had a chance to see and then think about what he'd written in the email.

"Hmm. Did you send an email? Um, yeah, when did you do that, again?"

Of course, there is forgiveness for these little mistakes we make in life. And he just laughed it off because he's a Christian man and a friend. Most often we all know to take these kinds of failures in stride and move along. And we hope others will give us the benefit of the same stride when we fall short. But it sure is a lot harder to stretch oneself to the extremities of Christian love and forgiveness when someone speaks or acts in a deliberately offensive way—when they speak ill of you, when they do something incredibly hard to undo let alone to forgive and forget. It's the nature of man to be scarred by such things, and then to reach back into the fray to reward damage for damage.

Still, living and serving together as a family in Christ means doing the opposite of what I described. It means at a bare minimum, forgiving, amending if possible, and then working diligently to do as God does: Forget it ever happened.

That's right. God forgets your sins.

> I am he who blots out your transgressions for my own sake, and I will not remember your sins. (Isaiah 43:25)

If you are in the mood for memorizing a new text from God's Word, that's one worth remembering. It's telling you just how complete God's forgiveness truly is. Maybe think of it this way. When you stand before God on the Last Day, if you try to bring up the sins you've committed in the past that have been covered by the blood of Christ and the forgiveness won on the cross, He's going to look at you and say, "I have no idea what you are talking about."

Perhaps one of the things we can take away from the celebration of Pentecost we just recalled yesterday is that by the power of the Holy Spirit, the strange forgetfulness of God's love is made known to us and the world. It's poured into us by the Holy Spirit, and with that, we are not only given the supernatural ability to acknowledge our failings in light of God's Law, but we can forgive the failings of people around us. Even further, we are empowered for some pretty amazing things in this life, things we never expected we'd be able to do.

Another example: After that interaction with the Trustee co-chair, I told him I'd reply to his email first thing in the morning. And I did.

Essentially, the original email was about, as I said, the current and future needs of the facility and how we might go about tackling them even as money is tight. In my response, I took a moment to mention that within the last six years, our congregation has almost completely changed the way she goes about her stewardship of Christ's gifts—namely the attention we give to prayerful giving. We've become more attuned to understanding how the Holy Spirit works in the Church when it comes to the needs set before the people of God. Mainly, one thing we've learned is that gimmicky fundraisers are just that, gimmicky, and they don't do anything for long-term spiritual growth in the people participating. In other words, they're not spiritual meat and potatoes that keep the body healthy. They're more like a diet of Twinkies. You can eat them, and they'll keep you alive for a little while, but in the end, you're not going to thrive.

To rise above this, we practice what Saint Paul preached.

When there's a need, we communicate it and then we urge one another by the Gospel to be the very people God has made us to be. When we do this, we meet the challenges every single time. And then as we continue to look back to observe the efforts, we can see that we continue to get better at doing it. We're not paralyzed by terror when the struggles come, but rather well-fed and sturdy from the good sustenance that God provides through Word and Sacrament for meeting all things head-on.

I like that. But even if I didn't, it doesn't matter. It's how God works, plainly and simply.

God works through His Gospel. By the Gospel of the forgiveness of sins in Jesus, we are re-created to be His people and to face off with the challenges that come our way, knowing that the only loss in any challenge is death—and even then, to die in Christ is victory!

I suppose I began this by sharing about the incredible power to forgive one another. Living in this forgiveness, the final takeaway can be to know God's people are in the messes together as a Christian family. We listen to Him together, knowing He loves His people.

Be encouraged by that, and know He won't let you down.

✠

Guard Your Steps

I myself will be the shepherd of my sheep, and I myself will make them lie down, declares the Lord God. —Ezekiel 34:15

P lainly and simply, we are blessed to be God's people. We have nothing to offer Him and yet He continually reaches to us in love by His Gospel so that we would know exactly what that love looks like. It is fully seated in the person and work of His Son, Jesus Christ, who atoned for the sins of the whole world— *the whole world*. And then what is equally astounding is that He keeps the promise He made in Ezekiel 34 where He said:

> And I will bring them out from the peoples and gather them from the countries, and will bring them into their own land. And I will feed them on the mountains of Israel, by the ravines, and in all the inhabited places of the country. I will feed them with good pasture, and on the mountain heights of Israel shall be their grazing land. There they shall lie down in good grazing land, and on rich pasture they shall feed on the mountains of Israel (vv.13-14).

All of this talk of "the mountains of Israel" is a reference to worship. It is referring to the reality that as members of God's family, in a sense, we are lifted up and out of the world around us and set apart—which is literally what the word "holy" means. It means set apart. In holiness, God Himself feeds His holy people. He takes care of us. He makes His presence in our midst and shepherds us. And this can't be overstated. God says over and over throughout this particular section that He is the mover and not us. "I will," He repeats. And He emphasizes His point when He declares "I myself." He does that in both verses 15 and 16:

I myself will be the shepherd of my sheep, and I myself will make them lie down, declares the Lord God. I will seek the lost, and I will bring back the strayed, and I will bind up the injured, and I will strengthen the weak…

This text draws us to see Psalm 23 in a very clear way. The Lord is indeed our shepherd and we shall not want. He makes us lie down in green pastures. He leads us beside still waters. He restores our souls.

God is good.

Knowing all of this, the Old Testament writers set the stage for us to understand that when we come into the presence of God in holy worship, there is something, in particular, we ought to be ready to do. No, it isn't necessarily to sing His praises, although that does come as a natural response to the Gospel of our forgiveness. And no, it isn't to get so comfortable in His holy dwelling that we kick our feet up on the pews like we're at the movies or make a lot of racket in the nave before, during, or after the service. The "doing" is described by Solomon in Ecclesiastes 5:1-3 as being displayed through a particular demeanor:

> Guard your steps when you go to the house of God. To draw near to listen is better than to offer the sacrifice of fools, for they do not know that they are doing evil. Be not rash with your mouth, nor let your heart be hasty to utter a word before God, for God is in heaven and you are on earth. Therefore let your words be few. For a dream comes with much business, and a fool's voice with many words.

Solomon urges believers to guard their steps when entering into God's house, that is, we are humble, reverent, and meditative. And then poised with that demeanor, we are ready to listen—to hear and receive His Word, which is the food given in the good grazing land—rather than to prattle on with a less-than-tuned heart, mind, and spirit so that getting the most of our time in the Lord's presence is jeopardized.

Believe it or not, many churches have an actual room designed to remind and teach this very important truth. It's called the narthex. It's the room you pass through on your way from the lobby to the nave. The word narthex comes from the Greek word "narthekas," which means to purge. The narthex is that space between the outside world and the grazing land into which God is calling and setting us. It is that space where we can begin to shake loose the noise and distraction to "guard our steps." It is a place to begin the quiet reverence and meditation that is to be maintained in the nave— before, during, and after the service.

It's also that place where we can go—child or adult—to recalibrate when we just can't shake those things loose. And speaking of kids, it's the perfect spot to take the fussiest of our little ones (who are simply doing what children do) to settle them while still keeping them close to the action and eventually get them back into the house and into the presence of their Savior—where they belong!

Again, God is good. His Word declares this. And we, His people, know this. As we make our way into His holy house for worship every time it is offered, give thanks to Him and be at peace knowing that He will calm and comfort you, and He will give you all that is required for meeting a not-so-calm and not-so-comforting world beyond the doors of His Divine Service!

✟

In a World of Uncertainty

Surely he has borne our griefs and carried our sorrows. —Isaiah 53:4

W hen tragedy strikes, we learn what it means to wrestle with the otherworldly things.

Take, for example, the school shooting in Parkland, Florida—an event in which a gunman opened fire, killing seventeen people. When we heard the news—as a nation, as a community, as individual members of the fellowship of human depravity—we found ourselves shaken. Together, our guts were turned inside out as we watched the newscasts, read the articles, saw the images—the terrible images. One weeping parent's outstretched arms received her child with thankfulness while another parent winced and collapsed, embracing the pavement of the crime scene's perimeter, having just learned her child is gone—snatched away so violently, so unjustly, so unfairly.

And what are we to do in these moments? Just like you, I ask myself this question. Of course, as a Christian, I know that God is the only One to whom we can turn. We do so in prayer. And this is good. But it is something that happens most often while we're alone. We turn to our God in worship, too. We receive there the gifts that sustain not only for the good times but also, and perhaps most importantly, for the bad. And we do it together. We stand beside one another, not necessarily knowing the deepest concerns, but more than able to admit to being equals in this world before God.

This is good, because even as we gather before him in the unified confession of our sins, we leave His presence as a holy people, justified by His grace, empowered by the Holy Spirit with hope, and enabled to endure in a world of uncertainty, sorrow, and pain.

There's a lot to be mined from this divine reality.

The faith that is comprised of these things has eyes that are open to see what the world cannot see. It has ears to hear what the world cannot hear. It has a heart that is willing to admit to what is truly happening in this world and what is at stake.

I speak this way having participated in a press conference recently in which I stood beside a group of fellow Christian pastors in support of another pastor who's received death threats from the LGBTQ community for, in essence, his biblical stance on sexuality. No, I am not in fellowship with this man theologically. He and I have very different views on any number of theological things. And I can say the same of a majority of the Christian pastors who stood there at the podium in solidarity. But that wasn't the point. The point is that we have a common, external goal that involved protecting a Christian pastor's freedom to submit to and ultimately proclaim the Word of God as the standard for faith, practice, and life in this world.

But here's the more simplified take-away of my participation in the press conference as it relates to the events in Parkland, Florida: If we as a society are willing to allow (and perhaps even applaud) any community to threaten another in such ways over such things— for what amid common discourse would be considered differences of opinion—should we be surprised when the society's children kill one another? Something else is behind this. So much more is going on.

Still, we're asking, "What do we do?"

Might I suggest going to church? And taking the children along? Heed the biblical mandate to be present in the house of God to confess your participation in sin. Be absolved of your failings, and then receive more and more of His blessed forgiveness by the

Gospel gifts that can preserve you through this world's darkness. Don't look upon your time with God in holy worship as something so easily traded away for anything else in this life, no matter what it may be. Everything else is transient, and in an instant can be snatched away. Eternal life is just that: Eternal. Be immersed in the Word of God proclaimed and the Sacrament of Christ's body and blood administered for the forgiveness of sins. I'm certain that God will open your eyes in ways that such tragedies won't surprise you, but also, they won't overwhelm you to the point of uncertainty or despair. Instead, you'll be equipped to grieve for and with others. You'll be able to shine the light of Christ to those who need it. And if—God forbid—such a tragedy happens to you and your family, you'll most certainly mourn deeply, but not as one with no hope. I'd be willing to bet that same hope will burst into a bright-burning pyre in others in your Christian family, folks who will wrap their arms around you, who will come down to you in your sadness, who will point you to the One who has borne your grief and sorrows in a way that certifies them as temporary and never permanent.

God grant this to you.

✞

The Riptide of Busy-ness

Remember the Sabbath day, to keep it holy.   —Exodus 20:8

T he days seem to come and go so quickly. Considering that many among us plan our schedules by the minute rather than by the day, all of the events that land on our calendars with the intent of consuming our time sometimes leaves us thinking that life feels a little more like a rip current—a turbulent flow carrying us away from shore even as we try to swim against it— rather than a sometimes slow and sometimes fast stream that provides for both leisure as well as challenge. I read an article last week about how this is affecting children. In it, the author said:

> For years now, a consensus has been emerging that a subset of hard-driving, Ivy-longing parents is burdening their children with too many soccer tournaments, violin lessons and cooking classes. A small library of books has been published with names like *The Over-Scheduled Child, The Pressured Child, Pressured Parents, Stressed-Out Kids* and so on.

A little further into the article, he suggested a solution:

> The antidote to the problem… is to make sure children have enough time with no activities, parents have enough time with no work and the two sides come together to create activities of their own.

As I read this, I couldn't help but think that God provided the solution to this problem long before the clinical child psychologists ever started pondering it.

Take a look at the following portion from *Luther's Large Catechism* regarding the meaning of the Third Commandment, which is, of course, "Remember the Sabbath Day by keeping it holy."

> To offer ordinary people a Christian interpretation of what God requires in this commandment, we point out that we keep holy days not for the sake of intelligent and well-informed Christians, for these have no need of them. We keep them, first, for the sake of bodily need. Nature teaches and demands that the common people—man-servants and maid-servants who have attended to their work and trades the whole week long—should retire for a day to rest and be refreshed. Secondly and most especially, we keep holy days so that people may have time and opportunity, which otherwise would not be available, to participate in public worship, that is, that they may assemble to hear and discuss God's Word and then praise God with song and prayer.

I think it's kind of interesting, too, that in the very next Commandment, the Fourth Commandment—which deals with the honor due to parents as Godly authorities—after some pretty lengthy instruction for children, Luther turns toward the parents and writes:

> Parents should consider that they owe obedience to God, and that, above all, they should earnestly and faithfully discharge the duties of their office, not only to provide for the material support of their children, servants, subjects, etc., but especially to bring them up to the praise and honor of God. Therefore do not imagine that the parental office is a matter of your pleasure and whim. It is a strict commandment and injunction of God, who holds you accountable for it.

When you put these two commands together, first you see the one particular time and place that God has given for us to rest and be refreshed together as a family—holy worship. And second, you see how important it is to God that parents would be faithful in setting aside all of the busy-ness that would distract from or take priority over being together as a family and keeping the Sabbath day holy. A thorough reading of both explanations of these commands and you'll more than see the urgency for doing this, not only for the sake of rest but for the sake of establishing the right foundations for faith.

God knows the world tries to pull us into the rip current. He knows that if we try to swim against the current, we'll become exhausted. With this, He has given His Son to die and rise for us, giving us the Holy Spirit through the Gospel to see that there's a way out. In a real rip current, to escape isn't that hard. You need only to swim to the right or the left of it. In this life, getting what God has for your refreshing and re-strengthening isn't that hard, either. It happens every Sunday. And what's even more amazing is that to be in holy worship is to be lifted up and out of the rip current completely. You don't do any swimming. He does all the work. There in worship, you are rescued, you are set on shore, you are given dry clothes—the robe of Christ's righteousness—and you are well-nourished for the next wave that may come and try to sweep you away. If you and your children don't receive this nourishment, if you try to swim without what God provides, you will drown. That's the hard truth.

By God's grace, be encouraged to be with Him in His presence to receive this nourishment as often as it is provided. He loves you, and He wants for you to be refreshed alongside your resting Christian family.

✝

Uh-oh. Now What?

Do not be anxious about anything, but in everything, by prayer and petition, with thanksgiving, present your requests to God. —Philippians 4:6

It was a joy for my congregation to receive the proclamation of the Gospel from Pastor Jakob Heckert recently. Although, because of his late-stage cancer, we had to do it by way of a pre-recorded video. You see, we're not exactly a technologically advanced congregation. Although I'm confident that all in attendance were able to hear the Word, and that God's people were edified by the love of Christ proclaimed through their dear friend and pastor.

I'll admit I was concerned as to how well the sound would work in a room full of people. Even though I'd already spent a lot of time working with the audio stream in the video, I just didn't feel comfortable with it. And then the unthinkable...

When I arrived at the church the morning we were to view the sermon, I went into the nave to do one more test drive of the video. I discovered that the video file wasn't working as before. Somehow the file on the flash drive I had plugged into the Blu-ray player had become corrupted, and so the image was jittery and the audio was the same. I don't know what happened, but it was what it was.

Needless to say, I started to sweat because while my video camera is pretty decent—recording in HD—it's no small thing to go back and convert the HD MTS video files it creates into MPEG-2 files we can actually watch on the DVD/ Blu-ray player available to us. Not to mention I would need to boost the audio and do some processing to remove a strange hissing sound that could be heard in the recording I took while I was at Pastor Heckert's house doing the original video. With the acoustics of our church, the hissing sound made the video almost unwatchable.

But there is a lesson to be learned in all of this.

Even as I started to worry, I knew I'd need to get in gear and start the whole process all over again. And so I prayed. It was a short prayer, one I said as I jogged back to my office. I think it went something like this: "Heavenly Father, this is not good. You're gonna need to intervene here—big time—because I can only make my computer process at certain speeds and I don't have much time. I'm in a mess. Help. Please. I ask this in Jesus' name. Amen."

With that, I got to work on it right away, and after about an hour and a half, I had a video that, in my opinion, was far better than the first. Imagine that. In other words, what had unfolded as a nightmarish scenario, God used for good, and from it, I believe a better sermon video was produced. That had me thinking about something Saint Paul wrote.

> Do not be anxious about anything, but in everything, by prayer and petition, with thanksgiving, present your requests to God. And the peace of God, which transcends all understanding will guard your hearts and your minds in Christ Jesus. (Philippians. 4:6-7)

You know, the above words apply to more than just last-minute crunches like the one I described. These words, inspired by the Holy Spirit, cut to the heart of who we are in the midst of a fallen world. There's plenty out there to cause us to worry—sickness, messy finances, broken relationships, you name it—but God has given us a promise that He will hear our prayers, and He will act according to His good and gracious will, all of which leads to our salvation. That's what Paul means here. In a cold world, God's holy will for our eternal future will produce peace like a super-heated fire burning in the furnace of our souls. It will warm us to the knowledge of His ever-present love—to the knowledge that He will always have a care for us. And what is that peace? It is the peace proclaimed by the angels to the shepherds in Bethlehem—peace between God and man, peace located in the person and work of Jesus Christ, the Savior of the world.

My prayer to God for you this day is that no matter the challenges you may be facing—big or small—trust your Savior. Pray to Him. He loves you, and He loves to listen to you. And whatever He does to help, just know that it will be worked for your good according to His will. That's a peaceful thought. In fact, it's more than a thought. It's a piece of powerful knowledge and comforting reality worked by the Holy Spirit through the Gospel message. Hear it often. Receive it with joy, knowing that you mean so much to your God.

⊬

Losing is Hard

But I say to you who hear, love your enemies, do good to those who hate you, bless those who curse you, pray for those who abuse you. —Luke 6:27-28

I've never participated in the circulation of memes mocking folks who said they'd leave the country if a particular candidate won an election. Concerning Donald Trump's election in 2016, Whoopi Goldberg and Bryan Cranston come to mind.

I didn't participate in the web-wide prodding of these two celebrities, and not because I wanted Whoopi and Bryan to stick around. Between you and me, I happen to think that dear Lady Liberty would be much better off if she weren't always scratching at her celebritous fleas. Still, I never participated because, quite simply, I was dealing honestly. I know how hard it is to lose. I know what it's like to have a long-suffering and hopeful expectation for victory building in momentum throughout what feels like a calendar-consuming "forever" suddenly become something else in a little more than an hour of election result postings.

Losing is hard. It hurts terribly. And if one is not careful, it can negatively recalibrate so much more than emotions. It can lead to some of the deeper, darker places that would see words spoken between people—between families, friends, and neighbors—and to have those relationships broken beyond repair.

Losing is hard. Forgiveness—real, down in the filth forgiveness—is too. Look to Christ on the cross and measure the effort to win our forgiveness. It wasn't easy. It was hard. Now, I'm not talking about the perfect love that put Him there. It's God's innermost nature to love us and want to save us. It's His alien work to punish. In His truest nature, when God looks upon us, He does so in love. I mean, when Adam fell into sin, He didn't crash down with a thundering voice, "What have you done?" But instead, He called out, "Where are you?" His first work was to find us in our shame and bring us back. Of course, human love doesn't even come close to this perfect love. It's tainted, and it doesn't guarantee forgiveness. I can, in a sense, love a friend, and yet never be rid of the gnat-like memories of the times they've hurt me. Forgiveness, like losing, is hard.

But by God's grace, and perhaps strangely, there is the opportunity before so many of us to see that losing and forgiveness walk in stride. Losing means someone else stands above us on the pedestal in victory. Forgiveness means putting aside selfish pride to be the victor and existing in humility below another, too. I dare say that with forgiveness as the focal point of losing's horizon, things can and will be okay.

✝

There's No Place Like Home

If anyone loves me, he will keep my word, and my Father will love him, and we will come to him and make our home with him. —John 14:23

Vacations are nice. Still, it's always good to come home. Knowing the significance of what is meant by the word "home," the Lord points out in John 14:23 that when it comes to the places and relationships we possess in this life, our church home is to be considered precious.

First of all, God has established holy worship as the where-and-when of His coming to be with us through His verbal and visible Word. Secondly, those who love the Lord and keep His Word—that is, the baptized believers—are the ones God calls His family.

Do you want to know something else? Another part of what makes your church a place to call "home" is you. There's nothing better than a familiar face and a kindly embrace welcoming you back since last week, last month, or last year. There's nothing better than a kind word that is sure to let you know that while you were gone, you were missed. Whenever I go away for a short time, upon my return, the people of my congregation are sure to greet me this way. When they do, it reminds me just how wonderful being home can be.

I suppose this moves me to encourage you to count your own church as your home, as well. The people there are your Christian family. You belong there. And no matter what you've done, your church is to be a place where those who are repentant will always be received—and not only by our gracious and loving Savior, but by those within whom the Holy Spirit is at work by that same Gospel of overarching grace.

Grace.

This, of course, means that none of this is true by anyone's own doing, just as no one chooses their family. They are born into it. Similarly, you were born into the Christian community through baptism into Christ, the One who gave Himself on the cross to win for you your place before the throne as an heir of heaven.

I think that's a wonderful thought, and I hope you think it's wonderful, too. It is a comforting Gospel that changes the way we deal with one another, and it strengthens all in the church family to be honest with one another—to recognize our common need for a Savior from sin, and then together as a family, to kneel before His throne of grace to be absolved of anything and everything that would cause us despair.

Again, that's pretty wonderful.

I guess one more thing that makes it truly spectacular is that because of the person and work of Jesus Christ, it's all free—free as the breeze that jostles the leaves on the tree in your backyard.

Breathe it in. It is your baptismal right as a member of your church family.

☩

Preach the Text

Preach the word; be ready in season and out of season; reprove, rebuke, and exhort, with complete patience and teaching. —2 Timothy 4:2

E arly this past Sunday morning before worship, I posted something on Facebook that stirred a few distant friends to respond by way of Facebook Messenger. The conversations were rather interesting. But before I share the basics of the interactions, let me share with you what I posted. Here it is:

> The Last Sunday in the Church Year. That final day of the Church's calendar when we lean forward in anticipation of the One who comes again in glory to judge both the living and the dead. I dare say it's very possible that if ever there was a day your pastor might be bold enough to preach things that bother the tepid and less-interested, it is today. "Go to church!" he might say. "Be fed by Word and Sacrament!" he may call earnestly. "It is by these Gospel means that you will be made ready." And then he'll add, "A day is coming when neither reasonable excuse nor deliberate rejection will be tolerated any longer." Tapping his finger upon the edge of the pulpit and jeopardizing the comfort of your friendship, he may be so daring to say, "The culture's mythology of a Lord who never judges will have run its futile course." And then with a posture that reflects the strangest mixture of both human joy and sadness, the truth will be given. "Those who are ready will be welcomed into the marriage feast of heaven. Behind them, the door will shut—never to be opened again."

> Go to church, folks. Listen to the preaching of both Law and Gospel. Divine love is being distributed there; one bit of love so kindly revealing a most desperate need, and the other a supernatural potency for knowing, believing, and confessing Christ—the Ruler of earth and heaven—the One who will return at an hour unknown and say, "Come, blessed of the Father, and receive the inheritance prepared for you from the foundation of the world," or "Away from me, for I never knew you."

Go to church. By the power of the Holy Spirit, refill your vessel with oil. Trim your lamp. Be ready for the bridegroom. The day is surely drawing near.

Late yesterday afternoon, I got a few notes from folks about the message. There was one in particular that stood out the most. It was from a fellow pastor who, even as he resonated with the message's contents, was concerned that I'd overweighed the Law at the expense of the Gospel.

Maybe I did. Maybe I didn't. For one thing, I'm not all that interested in preaching sermons that follow a particular formula. That is, as I've shared with the folks in my Sunday morning adult Bible class, I don't necessarily make plans to tell of you off for five minutes and then tell you how it'll be okay for another five. Some guys come to the preaching task thinking of Law and Gospel in that way. I don't. I'd rather preach the text and let the Law and Gospel chips already inherent to the Scriptures fall where they may. It's already there. If I preach the text, it will show up in just the right amounts—just as God would have it preached. And I told my friend as much. But what was most interesting about the conversation was that he said, "I wouldn't have said it the way you did, but I'm more than happy to let you be the one to do it."

I wasn't sure what to make of that comment, but I sense that he thinks what I wrote was needed. He just didn't want to be the one to say it. I think that's true for a lot of folks. Most often we'd prefer to let others say what needs to be said than to actually say it ourselves.

There's no way to get around it, folks. The core of the Gospel reading for the Last Sunday in the Church Year is a warning to be ready. And if those who are called to stand in the stead and by the command of Christ won't preach it, who will?

And why does this matter, anyway? Well, I suppose it's the same as asking why we would need warnings in general. I can't help but think that for the most part, warnings are good, not bad. They communicate to us that something is lurking to our detriment, and in kindness, there is the desire to give us the information we need to avoid it. With that, I don't necessarily see a warning as unloving—and not necessarily even overly weighting of the Law. Certainly, the seriousness of their nature can be hard to iterate and uncomfortable to share. Depending upon the type of warning required, a lot may be risked when you warn someone. Still, when it comes to eternal life, the warning of God's Law is a loving revelation that works in tandem with the Gospel. It doesn't give the Gospel its power for conversion of the heart, but it certainly sets the stage in a way that allows the Gospel to shine. In other words, if the seriousness of the bad news is excluded, what care is there for the glory of the Good News? If I don't know I'm in danger, what care do I have for the One who came to rescue me?

In the end, I hope that the words I choose to use are effective. Rest assured that I pray before I write anything that is intended to communicate the Word of God in a public way. I ask the Lord to use my fingers as I type, to guide my speech, to put all of the words not just in the right order, but in the best and most powerful order. With that, I often find that the fear that sometimes comes with saying what needs to be said will often dissipate into the atmosphere like raindrops in the summer sun.

God calls for faithfulness. But He only does so when and where He promises to provide all that is necessary to make faithfulness possible. And that makes the job of telling both the harder news and the easier news a little less terrifying.

✝

www.ingramcontent.com/pod-product-compliance
Lightning Source LLC
Chambersburg PA
CBHW021142090426
42740CB00008B/894